LEARNING TO HEAR GOD'S VOICE

LEARNING TO HEAR GOD'S VOICE

KEN KESSLER

Restoration Times Publications, Inc.
Kennesaw, Georgia, U.S.A.
www.RestorationTimes.net

Learning to Hear God's Voice.

Copyright © 2003 by Ken Kessler.

Published by:

    Restoration Times Publications, Inc.
    P.O. Box 671063
    Marietta, GA 30066-0136
    http://www.restorationtimes.net

Printed and bound in the United States of America. All rights reserved. Written permission must be secured from the publisher to use or reproduce any part of this book, except for brief quotations in critical reviews or articles.

Italics in biblical quotes indicate emphasis added.

Unless otherwise noted, Scripture quotations are from the *New American Standard Updated (NASU) Edition*. Copyright © 1960, 1962, 1963, 1968, 1971, 1972, 1973, 1975, 1977, 1995 by the Lockman Foundation. Used by permission.

Other Scripture quotations are from the *New King James Version*, copyright © 1982, Thomas Nelson, Inc.

Cover design: Junxure Creative, Inc. (www.junxure.net)
International Standard Book Number: 0-9745235-0-X

Printed by Morris Publishing
3212 East Highway 30
Kearney, NE 68847
1-800-650-7888

Contents

Preface		7
Introduction		11
Chapter 1	Called Into Fellowship with God	15
Chapter 2	Intimacy with God: The Foundation for Hearing God's Voice	25
Chapter 3	Discerning God's Voice	41
Chapter 4	Ministering As Jesus Did	59
Chapter 5	Hearing God for Ministry	76
Chapter 6	Keys to Hearing God's Voice	102
Chapter 7	The Baptism of the Holy Spirit	119
Chapter 8	The Gift of Tongues	141
End Notes		161
Recommended Reading		162
About the Author		163

Preface

My sincere desire is that the Holy Spirit will use this book to impact your life. I hope it will stir and equip you as one who hears God's voice. God desires to speak to all of His children, not just to the preacher or a few special leaders. Most of all, God desires to speak to you.

I have been on a journey of learning to hear the voice of God since the early 1980's and have been leading our church down this path since 1991. This book is the result of what I have gleaned. The principles that I share in this book were learned the hard way—through the exciting and painful adventure of first-hand experience. These principles are based upon what has worked for me. They have shaped my life and impacted the way I minister. As I think back over my walk with the Lord, these principles have given me great joy and have drawn me progressively toward a more intimate walk with Jesus. These truths have worked for me, and I know they will work for you as well.

I owe a special expression of gratitude to many people who helped me along this journey of learning to hear God. Even though I have never met most of these men and women of God, their writings and tapes have been invaluable to assist me in this exciting pursuit. Special thanks go to Jack Deere, Bill Hamon, John Wimber, and Len and Linda Reddick for their contributions to my life.

Before you read this book, I want to explain three things. First, I want to clarify how the word "hear" is used in the title and throughout the book. As you get into the book, you will realize that I not only write about hearing, but about seeing and feeling as well. Though this is true, I have used "hearing" as a general term that groups together all the different ways that God communicates to us. For example, we don't hear dreams or visions, we see them. We don't hear a feeling in our body, we feel it. Although this is true, I use the word "hear" as a generic term that embodies all the different forms that God uses to communicate with us. My reason is this: Our objective is to receive communication from God—for us to recognize His voice—regardless of how He speaks. Since we communicate with others by hearing what they say, I have used "hear" to imply how we communicate with God by recognizing His voice. Therefore, I will use the word "hear" to describe the information that we receive from God through a dream, a vision, a feeling, or any other form of communication.

Second, I have written this book to accomplish two goals. These are:

1. To help equip our Life School students to hear the voice of God
2. To help equip any believer to hear the voice of God

My main reason for writing this book is to compliment our Life School class entitled *Learning to Hear God's Voice*. In doing so, I have written each chapter to correspond to a teaching session in the class. For example, Chapter 1 relates to Session 1 in the class. Chapter 2 corresponds to Session 2 and so forth (there is more information about the Life School at the end of this book). My secondary reason for writing this book is to help any believer—whether or not they are enrolled in our Life School—to hear the voice of God. Therefore, I designed this book to be beneficial to all readers not associated with the Life School. This is a stand-alone book that will help anyone in the Body of Christ develop skills to hear the Lord's voice.

Third, in Chapters 7 and 8, I discuss my position on the baptism of the Holy Spirit and the gift of tongues in great detail. I have taken a somewhat different approach in these chapters than in the others. The reason I spend so much time explaining my position on these issues is because of the misunderstanding, confusion, and disagreement these gifts have created in the Body of Christ. To a large degree, the baptism of the Holy Spirit has created a major division between the Evangelical and Charismatic streams. In writing these chapters, I state my beliefs on these issues in order to help release believers into these gifts. My beliefs concerning these two subjects were developed over a number of years through personal experience and the teachings of the Bible. My goal in Chapters 7 and 8 is to present clear, Scriptural reasons why these gifts are vital to the Church. I want to breakdown every barrier that hinders God's people from receiving the baptism of the Holy Spirit and the gift of tongues. I want to exhort believers to pursue the release of these gifts into their lives.

Introduction

We live in an exciting generation. We are living in the last days and are fast approaching the time of the Lord's return. These are days of destiny for the Church. God is preparing a Bride for Jesus. He is transforming the Church into mighty warriors who can stand in spite of difficulties. He is equipping this army to do great exploits in Jesus' name. Although the end of the age will be fearful and challenging to the world, the Church will enter into her finest hour.

To be a person of destiny in these end-times, it is essential that we learn to hear God's voice. Being equipped to hear the Lord's voice is no longer a nice option for the hungry and spiritually advanced believer. To stand in the days ahead, each of us must learn to recognize His voice. Hearing from God will be vital to our survival as the days grow darker. It is also an indispensable tool for the End-Time Church and for true followers of Jesus Christ.

Jesus said, "My sheep hear My voice, and I know them, and they follow Me" (John 10:27). To truly follow Jesus we must recognize His voice. How can we know where Jesus is leading us unless we hear from Him? How do we know whom to marry or what job to take unless Jesus speaks to us? How can we minister effectively in God's advancing army without hearing Jesus, the commander-in-chief? To be a true follower of Jesus Christ, we must learn to hear His voice.

Not only does hearing from God enable us to follow Him, but it also fulfills a deep passion within the heart of

God. For thousands of years, the Father has yearned for a people that would find their greatest joy in listening to His voice. The Psalmist prophetically expressed this when he penned Psalm 81. Speaking through the Psalmist, God said:

> But My people did not listen to My voice, and Israel did not obey Me. So I gave them over to the stubbornness of their heart, to walk in their own devices. Oh that My people would listen to Me, that Israel would walk in My ways! I would quickly subdue their enemies and turn My hand against their adversaries. Those who hate the LORD would pretend obedience to Him, and their time of punishment would be forever. But I would feed you with the finest of the wheat, and with honey from the rock I would satisfy you (Ps. 81:11-16).

The Father longs for a company of people that will heed His Psalms 81 call. How He desires for us to wait in His presence and hear His voice! Look at the great blessings He promises those that make hearing from Him their top priority. He vows to defeat our enemies. He promises blessing, prosperity, and abundance. Before the Lord returns, the Father will fulfill the Psalms 81 call in His people. He will transform His people into listening servants that only do what He is saying.

Hearing from God is also a foundational principle that prepares us to accomplish three major works that God is emphasizing in our day. Hearing God's voice is necessary to:

- **Develop an intimate relationship with Jesus.** This is an essential part of the Worship Movement that is covering the earth today. It is also vital to the Church being prepared as a Bride for Jesus.

- **Minister as Jesus did.** This is the major way that the mighty army of worshipping warriors will fulfill God's will in this last hour of history.

- **Become a significant member of the company of praying intercessors.** In the days prior to the Lord's return, God is appointing a mighty band of prayer warriors who will partner with God to see His will accomplished in the earth. In His sovereignty, God has chosen to work through people. A major way He does this is through the prayers of His Church. We know that God hears us and answers us when we pray according to His will. However, to pray His will, we must know His voice.

Let me summarize these main points: To stand in the end-times, to follow Jesus wherever He goes, to satisfy the Father's desire for listening servants, and to fulfill these three major works of the Holy Spirit, we must learn to hear God's voice. This book is designed to help you do this. Throughout the book, I cover principles that I have learned on my own journey of recognizing God's voice. Because I have practiced these principles since 1991, I know from experience that they work. I have also seen them work effectively in the lives of the people I pastor and others throughout the world. By applying the principles in this book, the Holy Spirit will activate and sharpen the necessary skills required to know the voice of God. You will grow mightily in the ability to minister like Jesus did as you make these truths bone of your bone and flesh of your flesh.

Book Objectives

As we begin this book, I have seven objectives in mind. They are:

1. To convey effectively the truth that God desires to speak to every believer;

2. To build the faith, confidence, and expectancy within us that we are able to hear the voice of God;

3. To build a solid foundation of intimacy with God so that we are positioned to hear His voice;

4. To equip each of us with the necessary gifts, skills, wisdom, knowledge, and understanding so that we can recognize and discern the voice of God;

5. To magnify Jesus' method of ministry so that each of us will model our ministry after His;

6. To activate the nine gifts of the Holy Spirit in our lives so that we can minister like Jesus did;

7. To explain clearly the baptism of the Holy Spirit and the gift of tongues from the Scriptures and my own experience so that every barrier that hinders these valuable gifts from being fully released in your life is removed.

CHAPTER ONE

CALLED INTO FELLOWSHIP WITH GOD

My sheep hear My voice, and I know them, and they follow Me.

JOHN 10:27

Listen carefully to Me, and eat what is good, and let your soul delight itself in abundance. Incline your ear, and come to Me. Hear, and your soul shall live.

ISAIAH 55:2-3, NKJV

It was a warm spring day in 1984 and I was in my garage doing some spring-cleaning. Earlier in the morning, I had spent three hours in prayer as part of a discipleship class that I was teaching. At that time, Donna (my wife) and I had two boys, ages 12 and 7. We were both quite content with the size of our family and had no plans for more children. In fact, we were praying about permanent birth control measures. As I asked God about our plans, He really surprised me. He said to trust Him and have more children! What a shock! I thought, "How am I going to tell Donna about this?" She was content with two children. Her lifestyle was getting easier as the children grew older. Alone, sweeping the garage floor, many thoughts raced through my mind. Was this really God speaking or was this just my imagination? Are we too old to have more children? How would I explain this to Donna?

I was pretty sure that I had heard God's voice. As these thoughts flooded my mind, a long-time friend pulled into our driveway. She had borrowed our baby bed several years before when she and her husband were expecting a baby. Two children later, she drove up with—you guessed it—our baby bed in her car! Totally unsolicited by either Donna or myself, she brought the bed back and said, "I am bringing your bed back. You might need it." At that point I knew! This couldn't be a coincidence. God had spoken to me and we were to have more children. Our third son, Jonathan, was born in 1986 and our fourth son, Stephen, in 1989. It has been about twenty years since that day in the garage and we now have four boys. Jonathan and Stephen are both teenagers and are a tremendous blessing to our family. What a blessing it has been that God spoke those words to me that morning, and that I took the time to listen.

From this event, I realized God's sheep hear His voice and that God desires to fellowship with man. We see this demonstrated in the Garden of Eden as God spoke freely to Adam and Eve, walking with them in the cool of the day. He had fellowship with them. He communicated with them. Adam and Eve were friends of God. Not only was this true in the garden, but also throughout history, God and man have had fellowship. Through this fellowship, God has nurtured, loved, and guided man. God has also invited man to partner with Him in advancing His kingdom throughout the earth.

Intimate fellowship with God is the foundation of our Christian experience. Jesus Christ came to earth to offer us much more than a dead religion—He invited us to become the friends of God. Christianity, therefore, is a personal relationship based on fellowship between God and His people. Paul stated this when he said, "God is faithful, through whom you were called into *fellowship* with His Son, Jesus Christ our Lord" (1 Cor. 1:9). Fellowship implies a partnership of two-way communication, joint participation, intimacy, and communion.

We all know that for communication to be effective between two people, it must include talking and listening. One-way communication that is dominated by one person talking while another listens is not nearly as fulfilling as two-way conversation. This same principle is true in our relationship with God. For our relationship to grow and be fulfilling it must be two-way. Most believers are far more comfortable doing all the talking and little of the listening. Our prayers consist of a list of needs and wants, yet we often spend very little time listening to what God desires to speak. However, listening to God's voice is an essential part of our relationship with Him. Note these Scriptures:

> While he was still speaking, a bright cloud overshadowed them, and behold, a voice out of the cloud said, "This is My beloved Son, with whom I am well-pleased; *listen* to Him!" (Matt. 17:5).

> My sheep hear *My voice*, and I know them, and they follow Me (John 10:27).

> But He answered and said, "It is written, 'MAN SHALL NOT LIVE ON BREAD ALONE, BUT ON EVERY WORD THAT PROCEEDS OUT OF THE MOUTH OF GOD'" (Matt. 4:4).
>
> He who has the bride is the bridegroom; but the friend of the bridegroom, who stands and *hears* him, rejoices greatly because of the bridegroom's voice. So this joy of mine has been made full (John 3:29).
>
> Listen carefully to Me, and eat what is good, and let your soul delight itself in abundance. Incline your ear, and come to Me. *Hear*, and your soul shall live (Isa. 55:2-3, NKJV).

From these passages, it is evident that God desires fellowship with each of us. He loves to hear our voice as we worship and pray. He enjoys it when we talk to Him about our concerns, fears, hopes and dreams. And He eagerly desires us to be attentive to His voice as He speaks words of encouragement, love, nurture and guidance.

Why We Need to Hear God's Voice

There are at least three reasons why we need to learn to hear God's voice for ourselves. Each of these reasons strengthens our relationship with God and draws us closer to Him. Hearing God's voice:

1. Builds intimacy and friendship with Jesus
2. Gives us personal guidance
3. Is essential for effective ministry

1. **Hearing God's voice builds intimacy and friendship with Jesus.**

Hearing Jesus' voice is one of the most fulfilling parts of a personal relationship with Him. When He speaks affectionate words to us or when He gives us revelation and guidance, it encourages and draws us closer to Him. We feel loved and secure in our position in Him. Even if He has just spoken a word of correction to us, we feel cherished and close to Jesus just because He—the God who created the universe—spoke to us. Hearing His voice nurtures an intimate and loving friendship with Him. This is such an important topic that we have devoted an entire chapter to discuss it. In Chapter 2, we will look at how cultivating an intimate relationship with Jesus is the foundation for a lifestyle of hearing His voice.

2. **Hearing God's voice gives us personal guidance.**

We need to learn to hear God's voice so that we can follow Jesus. For example, we know from the Bible that man is to work. Paul said, "If anyone will not work, neither let him eat" (2 Thess. 3:10). But we do not know from the Bible whether we are to work at the factory down the road or at the store in town. We need to hear God's voice in order to know which job to take. We also know from the Bible that God plans for most people to marry. God said, "It is not good for the man to be alone; I will make him a helper suitable for him" (Gen. 2:18). However, the Bible doesn't tell us whom to marry. We need to hear His voice so that we marry the right person.

I saw the importance of this in 1998 when my oldest son, Bryan, got engaged to his wife, Angie. She is the perfect helpmate for him and she is a wonderful daughter-in-law to us—

we love her very much. While they were dating, both Bryan and Angie believed that God wanted them to get married. However, they both wanted God to speak clearly to them in order to confirm this.

One day Bryan decided to give Angie a piece of jewelry to demonstrate his love for her. He asked his manager at work for a place to purchase quality jewelry. His manager recommended a jewelry store that Bryan had never been to. Before Bryan entered the store, he said a little prayer to God, "Lord, please show me what to buy." As he looked around the store, a cross pendant stood out to him so he decided to buy it. When he gave it to Angie later that night, she was in shock. She asked him, "Did you talk to anyone? Did you talk to my mom?" Bryan did not know why she was so surprised by the gift so Angie told him, "Three years ago I went to the same jewelry store with my mom and I saw a similar cross pendant. When I saw it, I said a little prayer to God, 'Lord, let the man that I marry buy this for me.'" God supernaturally revealed to them that they were to get married. What an exciting confirmation of God's voice to them! From this example, we see how important it is to hear God's voice for personal guidance.

3. Hearing God's voice is essential for effective ministry.

During the days of His earthly ministry, Jesus only did what He heard or saw His Heavenly Father doing. Jesus only healed when His Father said to heal. He only cast out a demon when He heard His Father say to do so. Jesus had a strong relationship with His heavenly Father that was uninterrupted by sin. Because of this, Jesus clearly heard from God and did His will. Likewise, we are called to do the same.

We must learn to hear our Father's direction and then do what He says do. Because this topic is so vital for effective ministry, in Chapter 4 we focus entirely on how Jesus ministered in response to hearing His Father's voice.

Common Ways God Speaks Today

God speaks to His people today in a variety of ways. Jack Deere, in his book *Surprised by the Voice of God,* presents four common ways that the Holy Spirit speaks today. He says that God speaks through:

1. The Bible
2. Experience
3. Natural means
4. Supernatural means[1]

1. God speaks through the Bible.

The most common way that God speaks to us is through the Bible. Paul said:

> All Scripture is given by inspiration of God, and is profitable for doctrine, for reproof, for correction, for instruction in righteousness, that the man of God may be complete, thoroughly equipped for every good work (2 Tim. 3:16-17, NKJV).

There are two Greek words for "word" in the Bible. One is *logos* and the other is *rhema.* When the word *logos* refers to the Bible, it corresponds to the general Word of God or the full counsel of God. The word *rhema* means the spoken word or a specific word of God spoken into a certain circumstance. God speaks to us through the written Word of God to give us a solid foundation for life. We will be blessed if we will become a doer of the "logos" Word of God. He also speaks through the specific "rhema" word in order to nurture us and provide specific direction for our life and ministry.

2. God speaks through experience.

Not only does God speak to us from the Bible, He also speaks through life experiences. He speaks through trials, through common events, through other people, and through miracles. Probably every one of us has had a friend speak a word of confirmation to us at just right moment. Most likely, we have also heard God speak in the midst of trials and difficulties about what really is important in our lives or to show us our need for patience and humility. God speaks often (and sometimes loudly!) through our experiences.

3. God speaks through natural means.

God also speaks through natural means. He speaks through nature. He speaks through the weather. He speaks through human messengers. We have all heard that perfect message from our pastor that was just right for us and spoke exactly into our circumstances. God also speaks through natural events. For example, several years ago when an earthquake hit San Francisco during the World Series, many believed God was speaking to the people of America to wake up. Through this devastating tragedy, many thought God was saying that playtime was over and that it was time for America to turn back to God.

4. God speaks through supernatural means.
God also speaks in supernatural ways. He speaks through dreams, through visions, through angelic encounters, through His audible voice, and through thoughts and impressions. We have found that many more believers have learned to discern the voice of God in the first three ways than in the fourth category. If believers can learn to hear God's voice through supernatural means, then they can become very effective at hearing God in each of the different ways that He speaks. Hearing God speak through supernatural means will be the primary emphasis of this book.

Become a Doer of the Word

God desires to speak to all of His children, not just to a special few. He is not just interested in speaking to the preacher, the president or the missionary. He desires to speak regularly and clearly to all who are in a relationship with Him. He is no respecter of persons. He will communicate with all who will dedicate themselves to learning to hear His voice. It takes time and attention to learn to hear God's voice. Furthermore, it is essential to understand that we cannot have true fellowship with our Lord Jesus Christ, nor can we do our part to advance His kingdom effectively, unless we learn to hear His voice. Therefore, I challenge you to make learning to hear God's voice a priority in your life!

As we conclude this chapter, it is important to remember the purpose of this book. It is to activate believers so that they might learn to be more effective in hearing God's voice. Since the principles taught in this book have proven successful in many different cultures and settings, they will also work for you. As we begin this study together, I exhort you to become a "doer of the Word" and not merely a "hearer only." In doing so, God will activate you to hear His voice more effectively, both for personal guidance and ministry!

CHAPTER TWO

INTIMACY WITH GOD: THE FOUNDATION FOR HEARING HIS VOICE

To accomplish much in God, we must obey His voice regularly. To obey His voice regularly, we must hear His voice repeatedly. To hear His voice repeatedly, we must have an ongoing lifestyle of intimacy with Jesus.

The title of this chapter describes an important principle in learning to hear God's voice. In fact, every other principle in this book hinges upon intimacy with God. Therefore, this truth is the most important concept that will be covered in the entire book. From my own experience, I neglected the importance of this truth for many years. When I first started teaching this material in 1991, I emphasized several other principles above intimacy with God. However, as time went on, I realized that a lifestyle of intimacy, fellowship, and communion with the Lord Jesus Christ is the most important aspect in hearing God's voice. This kind of lifestyle positions us to hear the voice of God with greater clarity and consistency. As we will see throughout the book, there are many important keys to hearing God's voice. However, without intimacy with God, we will only hear Him from a distance, and we will often miss Him when He speaks.

The Whisper of God's Voice

Most of us desire to hear the voice of God in powerful and dramatic ways. And sometimes God does speak in a spectacular fashion. However, God usually speaks in a quiet, soft voice—much like a whisper. Notice how Elijah heard the voice of God:

> And behold, the LORD passed by, and a great and strong wind tore into the mountains and broke the rocks in pieces before the LORD, but the LORD was not in the wind; and after the wind an earthquake, but the LORD was not in the earthquake; and after the earthquake a fire, but the LORD was not in the fire; and after the fire *a still small voice* (1 Kings 19:11-12, NKJV).

If we are distant from God, preoccupied with other things, it is very easy to be deaf to His whispers. Sometimes there are obstacles that block our ability to hear. In such cases, even though God may be speaking to us, we often can't hear His voice. It is much like two friends trying to carry on an important conversation. If they are far apart, they must shout to be heard. If the distance is far enough, it is difficult to hear even the shout. On the other hand, if they are close to each other, even a whisper is clearly heard.

We have been given many promises offering us a lifestyle of intimacy with God. As we act on these promises and draw near to God, we position ourselves to hear His voice—whether it comes as a shout or as a whisper. We are told in the Scriptures that the veil of separation has been torn asunder through the work of Jesus on the cross. Because of this, we can come boldly before His throne, have fellowship with God and be a friend of God in Christ. Because we are promised intimacy with God through the Lord Jesus Christ, we can live so close to God that we even hear His still, small voice.

How God's Servants Heard His Voice

Throughout Scripture, we see that God's servants performed amazing exploits only because they obeyed His voice. The only way that they could obey God's voice was to hear His voice. And the only reason they heard God's voice was because they were close to Him. This powerful principle is summarized below:

> To accomplish much in God, we must obey His voice regularly. To obey His voice regularly, we must hear His voice repeatedly. To hear His voice repeatedly, we must have an ongoing lifestyle of intimacy with Jesus.

We see this principle lived out in God's servants throughout the Scriptures. Let's look at the following six people in particular:

1. Jesus
2. Mary of Bethany
3. John the Baptist
4. King David

5. John the Apostle
6. New Testament Church

1. Jesus

Throughout the Gospel of John, we see that Jesus only did what He heard or saw His Heavenly Father doing. For example, note the following verses:

> Therefore Jesus answered and was saying to them, "Truly, truly, I say to you, the Son can do nothing of Himself, unless it is something He *sees* the Father doing; for whatever the Father does, these things the Son also does in like manner. For the Father loves the Son, and shows Him all things that He Himself is doing; and the Father will show Him greater works than these, so that you will marvel" (John 5:19-20).

> I can do nothing on My own initiative. As I *hear*, I judge; and My judgment is just, because I do not seek My own will, but the will of Him who sent Me (John 5:30).

> And in the morning, rising up a great while before day, he went out, and departed into a solitary place, and there prayed (Mark 1:35).

Jesus, the sinless and perfect Son of God, had an intimate relationship with the Father. He spent many hours in the presence of His Father in prayer. Out of this relationship, He heard the voice of the Father for ministry and for direction. As He heard God speak, Jesus obeyed and performed powerful miracles.

2. Mary of Bethany

In Luke 10:38-42, we read the story of Mary and Martha. Both of these women loved Jesus and welcomed Him into their lives. However, we see one major difference in the way they related to Him. Martha was busy—she was distracted from Jesus by doing things for Jesus. On the other hand, Mary took time to sit at the feet of Jesus to listen intently to His words. Because both of these women had different levels of spiritual intimacy, they also operated in different levels of spiritual power. We see evidence of this in John 11 when Lazarus died. Both Martha and Mary pleaded with Jesus to raise him from the dead. Jesus responded to Martha by giving her a great teaching about the resurrection. However, Jesus answered Mary's request by giving her a resurrection! It was Mary's plea that broke the heart of the Lord Jesus and motivated Him to raise Lazarus from the dead. The cry of one who had a lifestyle of intimacy with Him inspired the Lord to action.

3. John the Baptist

As recorded in Matthew 11:11, Jesus said that John the Baptist was the greatest of all people born up until that time. This was because of his role in preparing the way of the Lord. John's ability to prepare the way for the Lord's first coming was empowered by a lifestyle of intimacy. Read John's own testimony:

> He who has the bride is the bridegroom; but the *friend* of the bridegroom, who stands and *hears* him, *rejoices* greatly because of the *bridegroom's voice*. So this *joy* of mine has been made full (John 3:29).

Note the emphasized words in this verse. These words express John's lifestyle of intimacy with Jesus. John regularly heard His voice. This was John's greatest joy. He even called himself a friend of the Bridegroom. Because John was so intimate with the Lord, his ministry was powerful and effective in making ready a people prepared for the Lord. John's ministry was successful because he heard Jesus' voice regularly.

4. King David

We all know of the powerful ways that King David was used in the nation of Israel. He was a king after God's heart. He brought the Ark of the Covenant back to Zion. He established continuous worship before the presence of the Lord. He wrote many of the Psalms. Among his many outstanding characteristics, there were two that defined his life and positioned him to be used greatly of the Lord. First, he inquired of the Lord regularly and he obeyed what God said:

> Then David said to Abiathar the priest, the son of Ahimelech, "Please bring me the ephod." So Abiathar brought the ephod to David. *David inquired of the LORD*, saying, "Shall I pursue this band? Shall I overtake them?" And *He said* to him, "Pursue, for you will surely overtake them, and you will surely rescue all" (1 Sam. 30:7-8).

Second, David had an intimate relationship with God. David said:

> One thing I have asked from the LORD, that I shall seek: That I may dwell in the house of the LORD all the days of my life, to behold the beauty of the LORD and to meditate in His temple (Ps. 27:4).

David longed to be in the courts of the Lord. He hungered for the presence of God. Even though David made major mistakes, he had an intimate relationship with the Lord. Out of this relationship, he heard God's voice, and he obeyed.

5. John the Apostle

John the Apostle had an extremely close relationship with Jesus. We see this from the intimate snapshots that are scattered throughout John's Gospel. For example, in John 13:25, John is seen leaning against the heart of Jesus. In John 19:26, John refers to himself as the disciple whom Jesus loved. Out of this position of deep intimacy with the Lord, John received profound and powerful revelation. It was years later, when John was exiled for preaching the gospel, that his intimate friend visited him in an extraordinary way. John saw Jesus Christ unveiled in a way that no other human being has ever seen Him. John saw Jesus in His glorified, resurrected body. John saw the God-man in all of His majesty. Because John was intimate with the Lord, he was chosen to write one of the greatest books in history: The Revelation of Jesus Christ.

6. New Testament Church

Intimacy with the Lord, hearing His voice, and being used to advance the kingdom of God with power also characterized the early church. Note the following passage:

> Now there were at Antioch, in the church that was there, prophets and teachers: Barnabas, and Simeon who was called Niger, and Lucius of Cyrene, and Manaen who had been brought up with Herod the tetrarch, and Saul. While they were *ministering to the Lord* [intimacy] and fasting, *the Holy Spirit said*, "Set apart for Me Barnabas and Saul for the

work to which I have called them." Then, when they had fasted and prayed and laid their hands on them, they sent them away (Acts 13:1-3, emphasis mine).

The first century church had an intimate relationship with the Lord. They ministered to Him regularly through worship, prayer, and fasting. Out of this lifestyle, they positioned themselves to recognize God's voice. When God spoke to them, they obeyed and took the gospel throughout the earth.

From these six examples, we see that intimacy positions the believer to hear the voice of God. Let me repeat the important principle that we stated at the beginning of this section:

> To accomplish much in God, we must obey His voice regularly. To obey His voice regularly, we must hear His voice repeatedly. To hear His voice repeatedly, we must have an ongoing lifestyle of intimacy with Jesus.

Just as this principle applied to God's servants in the Bible, it also applies to us. Through the Lord Jesus Christ, we are called into a lifestyle of intimacy with God whereby we hear His voice and do what He says to do.

Why Intimacy Is So Important in Hearing God's Voice

Why is intimacy with Jesus so important in hearing His voice? The answer has to do with the way we are made. We are comprised of body, soul, and spirit (1 Thess. 5:23). With our body, we contact the physical world through our five senses. With our soul, we think, feel, and act. With our spirit, we relate to the Spirit of God. When we are intimate with Jesus, our spirit-man rises above our soul and we become more sensitive to the voice of God.

A strong, sensitive spirit is important in deciphering God's voice from the many voices that speak to us. For example, our senses speak to us through *cravings* for fulfillment, our mind speaks to us through *thoughts*, our will speaks to us through potential *choices* and our emotions speak to us through *feelings*. All of these areas pull us one way or another. It is very easy for us to believe that the cry of our senses or soul is the voice of God into our lives. However, the Word says that our spirit is the place where God speaks to us: "The spirit of man is the lamp of the LORD, searching all the innermost parts of his being" (Prov. 20:27). To discern properly the voice of God for our life and ministry, it is essential that we learn to distinguish the voices of the senses and soul from the voice of God in our spirit-man. Another verse of Scripture that will help us understand the importance of our spirit man becoming sensitive to God's voice is:

> But the natural man does not receive the things of the Spirit of God, for they are foolishness to him; nor can he know them, because they are spiritually discerned. But he who is spiritual judges all things, yet he himself is rightly judged by no one. For "who has known the mind of the LORD that he may instruct Him?" But we have the mind of Christ (1 Cor. 2:14-16, NKJV).

This passage tells us that we have the mind of Christ and that the things of God are spiritually discerned. How does intimacy with God fit into all of this? Intimacy with God feeds our spirit-man—nourishing our spirit and making us strong. As we pursue a lifestyle of seeking and abiding in the presence of God, our spirit-man arises. As our spirit-man arises, we begin to think more with the mind of Christ, and we discern the voice of God with greater clarity.

Let me summarize this. A lifestyle of intimacy with God causes our spirit-man to be nourished and strengthened. In turn, this causes our spirit-man to arise above our soul and body. When our spirit-man arises, we become more sensitive to the things of the Spirit and thereby hear the voice of God more clearly. Since our spirit is the place where God speaks to us, a strong spirit helps us discern between the voice of God and the voices that come from our mind, will, emotions, and senses.

Keys to Developing an Intimate Relationship with Jesus

Since intimacy with Jesus is so critical to hearing His voice, I want to finish this chapter by discussing practical ways to develop an intimate relationship with Jesus. It is important to understand that developing intimacy with Jesus is a lifelong process. It begins at the point of our salvation when we are declared to be in right standing with God through the blood of Jesus. From here, we are invited to come freely and boldly before His throne of grace. As we continue to come before God's throne on a regular basis, we will develop a lifestyle of intimacy with Jesus. Developing intimacy with Jesus is a continuous process that will be refined and cultivated throughout our entire life and walk with God.

Though intimacy with God is a lifelong process, there are some disciplines presented in the Bible that are necessary to cultivate this relationship. These disciplines will help us nurture a walk of intimacy with God. Some of these are:

1. Unconditional and ongoing surrender to the Lordship of Jesus Christ
2. Ongoing separation from the world's ways
3. Continuous separation unto God
4. Regular times of sitting at the feet of Jesus
5. Routinely ministering to the Lord

1. Unconditional and ongoing surrender to the Lordship of Jesus Christ

The concept of unconditional surrender is spoken of throughout the Old and New Testaments. Jesus said that we cannot be His disciples unless we deny ourselves, take up our cross daily, and follow Him (Luke 9:23). Many other passages speak of similar calls to surrender. Let me illustrate the importance of surrender in the development of intimacy in this way. Think of a man and woman who are dating. In the initial stages of the dating relationship, they may have many friends with whom they are equally open. But, as the relationship progresses toward engagement, they begin to confide in each other in a much deeper way, sharing the deep secrets of their hearts. Their relationship begins to take on a much higher degree of closeness, far surpassing any other relationship. As they enter the marriage covenant, their level of intimacy progresses to an even deeper level, as they become one in body, soul, and spirit. Although the emotional aspects of love are a major reason why the two have become so close, commitment is what actually binds them together. As both parties to the relationship become secure in the other's commitment to them, they begin to open up to the other in progressively deeper ways.

We also see this concept expressed beautifully in the Book of Esther. Esther was selected as a candidate to be the bride of King Ahasuerus. Because of her commitment and surrender to the leading of the king's eunuchs, she said "yes" to every part of the preparation process. Ultimately, this attitude caused her to be selected as queen. Because of her lifestyle, she was given the privilege to come freely into the king's presence and request anything she needed. Just as Esther grew closer to the king, we grow more intimate with the Lord as we continually surrender to the will and purposes of God. As we obey His voice, we grow closer to Him.

2. Ongoing separation from the world's ways

Throughout the Scriptures, Babylon is presented as a picture of what man is like apart from God. It often represents the independence and rebellion of man. It also symbolizes the ways of the world. In Revelation 18, Jesus tells His Church to come out of Babylon. At the time of His return, Jesus says that the voice of the Bride will not be heard in Babylon any longer. The Church as the Bride of Christ is a picture of how we relate to Jesus intimately.

From this picture, we can draw this principle: To grow in intimacy with Jesus, we must develop a lifestyle of progressive separation from worldly ways. James speaks along the same lines when he writes, "Do you not know that friendship with the world is hostility toward God? Therefore whoever wishes to be a friend of the world makes himself an enemy of God" (James 4:4). The Apostle John described worldly ways as the lust of the flesh, the lust of the eyes, and the boastful pride of life (1 John 2:16). Intimacy with the Lord grows as we separate from the lust of the flesh, the lust of the eyes, and the boastful pride of life. As we become those who are in the world but not of the world, our intimacy with God is enhanced.

3. Continuous separation unto God

Separation is a two-fold process. It requires separation from worldly ways as we discussed in the previous section, but it also requires a separation unto God. We are to not just separate from evil in order to be good. Rather, we are to separate from evil in order to be consecrated unto God and His purposes. Separation unto God is another important key to developing an intimate relationship with the Lord. Exodus 30:30 reads, "You shall anoint Aaron and his sons, and *consecrate* them, that *they may minister as priests to Me.*" Many times in Scripture, before God allows His people to minister to Him, He first calls them to a life of consecration. The Hebrew word translated *consecrate* means to be set apart for, to sanctify, to prepare, to dedicate, to be hallowed, to be holy, to be sanctified, to be separate, to devote. As we dedicate ourselves to God and His purposes, a deeper level of consecration comes about in our lives. As we embrace deeper levels of consecration, our intimacy with God grows.

4. Regular times of sitting at the feet of Jesus

After Martha complained to Jesus about Mary's inactivity,

Jesus told her that *sitting at His feet and listening to His words* was the only thing necessary in life (Luke 10:42). He told her that this one thing would never be taken away from her. Taking time to sit at the feet of Jesus—with a heart that seeks to know and respond to His Word—is an extremely important discipline that helps facilitate a lifestyle of intimacy with Jesus. Waiting on the Lord for Him to speak, with an attentive heart toward His voice, is vital if we want to grow closer to Him. If we want to know Jesus' voice better, there is really no short cut. It takes consistent times of sitting at His feet—with the Bible in hand—reading, meditating, and listening for His voice. To be intimate with the Lord, we must regularly break away from our busy schedules in order to wait on Him. Out of the practice of sitting at the feet of Jesus—reading, studying, meditating, and listening for His voice with a heart to obey—intimacy with God is developed.

5. Routinely ministering to the Lord

Ministering to the Lord is such a broad concept that it encompasses the four previous keys. Studying this truth throughout the Scriptures, we find that ministry to the Lord involves consecration—both separation from sin and dedication to God—along with the disciplines of worship, prayer, fasting, meditating on the Word and waiting on the Lord. In many cases, ministering to the Lord is set in the context of the Tabernacle of Moses or the Temple. In either case, ministry to the Lord is associated with progressing from the outer court, where ministry is focused on the people, to the inner court, where ministry is focused on the Lord.

The Tabernacle of Moses paints a beautiful picture of how we move toward the Holy of Holies and minister to the Lord. Each piece of furniture in the Tabernacle can symbolize an aspect of our relationship with God. The golden lampstand represents the Holy Spirit giving us light and revelation. The table of showbread is symbolic of the Word of God. The altar of incense typifies prayer and intercession. And the Ark of the Covenant is the place of God's glory and majesty. To minister to the Lord effectively, we need the ministry of the Holy Spirit, the Word of God, worship and prayer. As we practice these disciplines, we will grow closer to the Lord and abide in the presence of His glory.

We also see continuous ministry to the Lord around God's throne. As we glimpse the heavenly throne room pictured in Revelation 4-5, those that are closest to the Lord are continuously ministering to Him through praise, worship, and thanksgiving. Along the same lines, Acts 13 reveals how the early church ministered to the Lord and out of this, the Holy Spirit set apart Barnabas and Saul for ministry. Again, we note the relationship of intimacy to hearing God's voice. Through routine times of private and public ministry to the Lord, we develop intimacy with God that positions us to hear His voice.

Positioning Ourselves to Hear God's Voice

As we conclude this chapter, I can't emphasize enough the importance of the relationship between intimacy with God and hearing His voice. If we want to grow as people that discern His voice accurately, we must develop a lifestyle of intimacy with the Lord. As we establish these five keys for developing intimacy with the Lord, we will see results quickly. These results will increase over time, causing us to hear the voice of God clearly for devotional purposes, personal guidance and ministry effectiveness. As we give ourselves to the principles from this chapter, we will have the joy of intimacy with Jesus and we will position ourselves to hear His voice.

CHAPTER THREE

DISCERNING GOD'S VOICE

When he puts forth all his own, he goes ahead of them, and the sheep follow him because they know his voice. A stranger they simply will not follow, but will flee from him, because they do not know the voice of strangers.

JOHN 10:4-5

If you extract the precious from the worthless, you will become My spokesman.

JEREMIAH 15:19

As believers, there are many voices that speak to us. From Chapter 2, we saw that not only is God speaking to us, but also our own thoughts, wills, and emotions speak to us. We are bombarded by the voice of the world on a regular basis. And demonic spirits frequently whisper lies into our minds. Yet we know from the words of Jesus that His "sheep follow him because they know his voice. A stranger they simply will not follow, but will flee from him, because they do not know the voice of strangers" (John 10:4-5). To be effective in hearing God's voice for guidance and ministry, we must learn to discern the source of the voices that we hear. As God told Jeremiah, "If you extract the precious from the worthless, you will become My spokesman" (Jer. 15:19). To be people that hear from the Lord and speak for Him, we must extract the true word of the Lord from the other voices that clamor within us. In this chapter, we will look at two key factors that will help us do this.

THE CHARACTER OF GOD'S VOICE

When I began the journey of learning to hear the voice of God, I did not have a mentor. I came from a church that did not place a high priority on hearing God's voice. Instead, the emphasis was on reading and obeying the Bible. Although this is the most important aspect in hearing and obeying God, we still must hear the Lord speak to us personally. Jesus rebuked the Pharisees—who studied and obeyed the Bible rigorously—because they had never heard God's voice (John 5:37). So the Bible is foundational in hearing God, but we still must hear Him speak to our spirits.

As I pioneered through the unfamiliar territory of learning to hear from God, I had to learn by trial and error. I drew from a variety of classes and teachings. I listened to cassette tapes and went to different conferences. Although I learned a lot from these sources, it did not keep me from making my share of mistakes. In order to help us discern God's voice, I want to share one mistake I made several years ago. This example will highlight the necessity of understanding the character of God's voice.

One particular Sunday morning, we needed someone to help us out with praise and worship. Since our praise team would not be at church, we invited a lady from another ministry to fill in. This lady is a very sweet and anointed servant of God. We knew her very well from another ministry with which we had a good working relationship. At the time, she and her husband were trying to have children. They had been married for quite a number of years and had not yet conceived. At the end of the service—as we sometimes do when guests come to our church—we prayed for her. Our desire was to bless her and meet her needs. As we were ministering to her, a woman who was a member in our church began to speak "prophetically" over her. This woman—who has since left us—had quite a reputation for accurate prophetic insight. As she delivered the word, she told our guest worship leader that she and her husband would have a deformed child. She told them the reason for this was the amount of love that they could give the child. You can imagine the shock, discouragement, fear and anger this produced.

Months later, I woke up to what had happened. I called our guest, apologized to her, and asked her forgiveness. She was very gracious and willingly forgave. I prayed to break off any curse that the word might have released on her and her husband. A few years later, we received the good news that she had a baby—a perfectly healthy son. Praise the Lord for His mercy!

Although I didn't actually give this word, my mistake was in keeping silent. As the pastor, I did not bring the necessary correction after the word was given. My lack of correction indicated that I thought that the word was correct. Though this was a mistake on my part, we can learn many valuable lessons about distinguishing the voice of God from this example.

First of all, this word was not consistent with the character of God's voice. James 3:17-18 reads:

> But the wisdom from above is first pure, then peaceable, gentle, reasonable, full of mercy and good fruits, unwavering, without hypocrisy. And the seed of whose fruit is righteousness is sown in peace by those who make peace.

James said that God's wisdom has all of these attributes. Therefore, whenever God speaks, it will be:

- Pure
- Peaceable
- Gentle
- Reasonable
- Full of mercy
- Full of good fruits
- Unwavering
- Without hypocrisy

God's voice speaking into our lives will be consistent with His character and Word. From our example, not only was the word spoken by this woman not in line with God's character, it also brought discouragement and death. God's voice is just the opposite. He always speaks the best into our lives. His word brings life into our situation. Jeremiah 29:11 states, "For I know the thoughts that I think toward you, says the LORD, thoughts of peace and not of evil, to give you a future and a hope." God's voice will lead us by the still waters and restore our souls (Ps. 23). God's voice is also filled with kindness. Paul said, "It is the goodness of God that leads you to repentance" (Rom. 2:4). God's voice of kindness produces true repentance and holiness. God's kindness draws us to Him.

The voice of the Lord also builds us up and encourages us to continue on with God. Paul said, "But he who prophesies speaks edification and exhortation and comfort to men" (1 Cor. 14:3). Additionally, the voice of the Lord helps us to fight the fight of faith:

> This command I entrust to you, Timothy, my son, in accordance with the prophecies previously made concerning you, that by them you fight the good fight, keeping faith and a good conscience, which some have rejected and suffered shipwreck in regard to their faith (1 Tim. 1:18-19).

Now let's take a deeper look at the character of God's voice. What you hear should be consistent with God's character. Jack Deere in his book, *Surprised by the Voice of God*, presents several concepts about the character of God's voice. He states that God's voice: always agrees with the Scriptures; may contradict friends' opinions; has a consistent character; bears good fruit; is different from our voice; and is easy to reject.[1] From Deere's concepts and my own experience, I have listed some common traits about the voice of God. God's voice:

1. Always aligns with Scripture
2. Is filled with hope
3. Produces good fruit
4. Is quiet and soft
5. May come to us in ways that are easy to reject

6. Is not confined to our theological box
7. May differ from the opinions of friends or counselors
8. Should be accompanied by His peace

1. God's voice always aligns with Scripture.

God's voice may disagree with our interpretation of Scripture, but it will never disagree with Scripture. God will not speak something to us that is contrary to the Word. The Spirit and the Word will agree. Let me illustrate with an example that I have heard many times.

A Christian girl who desires to go on with God is married to a man who is very complacent in his walk with the Lord. She knows that neither she nor her family can reach their full potential in God unless her husband changes or she gets a new husband. After years of trying to make her marriage work, nothing changes. Suddenly she "hears" a word to divorce her husband and marry a more spiritual man with whom she can fulfill her destiny. In fact, she even knows the man that she is to marry. This man has been showing her a lot of interest at church. Although his advances seem innocent, she is being drawn to him more and more. For years, she has longed for a spiritual man like this. When she "hears" the voice say that he is to be her husband, she is filled with excitement. She can now fulfill her destiny in God! She believes that she is to divorce her husband and he is to divorce his wife, leaving his wife with the two children.

The problem in this illustration is that the Scriptures speak against divorce (this is not to say that there is never a biblical reason for divorce). She has not heard the voice of the Lord. Instead, she has heard the voice of her emotions speaking to her. God's voice will always agree with the Scriptures.

2. God's voice is filled with hope.

God's voice does not nag, whine or argue. It is not mean or condemning. When God speaks, it is calm, quiet, confident, and filled with hope. God's voice often calls us to change certain aspects of our life. He might encourage us to get free of bondage or to overcome a flesh pattern. He could also exhort us to get victory over a certain besetting sin or to surrender an area to Him.

At times, a believer struggling with some difficult issue might "hear" a voice implying that if they don' get victory soon, calamity will strike. Although God does warn those who continue to walk in open rebellion, He treats the sincere but immature differently. God will not speak some horrible consequence for those who are truly trying to follow the Lord, but are falling short in an area of life. God's voice empowers us with hope and redemption. His voice is reassuring, certain, and positive.

3. God's voice produces good fruit.

God's voice will produce good fruit. If we have a lifestyle of listening to God's voice and obeying it, we should have a life that exhibits the fruit of God's blessing and leadership. Proverbs 10:22 reads, "It is the blessing of the LORD that makes rich, and He adds no sorrow to it." Over time, hearing and obeying God's voice will produce the good fruit of blessing in our lives. It will put our individual life, family, job, and ministry calling in order. When God speaks, it will produce blessings that money can't buy. God's voice will produce prosperity in our lives. His voice will lead to blessing whereas other voices lead to strife, dissension, and failure.

When I was an associate pastor, there was a married couple in our church who believed they heard God on all sorts of issues. A day came when they believed God was telling them that the husband should quit work and go back to college. So he quit his job and started school. Their plan was to live by faith. The only problem was that the wife was a stay-at-home mom. So in a very short time they began to struggle financially. The church saw their need and began to help them out. This went on for a while. The couple was praising God, thinking that He was providing for them in response to their faith. The church began to get very weary supporting a family that was not working. Finally, the entire situation exploded and they went back to work.

They were not living by faith. Rather, they were living by the compassion and mercy of those around them. What they "heard" from God did not bear good fruit. Later, they came to the church and confessed that they had not heard God correctly. Everything ended fine; however, we all learned a valuable lesson. God's voice bears good fruit.

4. God's voice is quiet and soft.

At times, God will speak in a thundering way; however, the majority of the time God will speak in a still, small voice (1 Kings 19:11-12). His voice is quiet, soft, and easy to miss. As I said in an earlier chapter, there have been times when I heard God's voice in a thundering way. At those times, there was absolutely no doubt that I had heard from God. However, the most common way that God speaks to me is in a still, small, quiet voice. This forces me to listen very closely so that I do not miss what He is saying. At times, very profound words have come to me very softly—almost imperceptibly. God's voice will most often come as a whisper.

5. God's voice may come to us in ways that are easy to reject.

Frequently, God comes to us in ways that make it easy for us to reject Him. He came to us as a baby in a stable when we were looking for a prince on a white horse. He came to us as a sacrificial Lamb when we were expecting a reigning King. He came to us in the weakness of human flesh when we were anticipating the fullness of glory. Even now, He comes to us in a shadowy dream when we are looking for a solid text of Scripture. He only lets us prophesy in part and know in part (1 Cor. 13:9) when we want complete understanding. Each of us must be very careful to listen for the voice of God—no matter what source it comes from.

Let me share two illustrations to explain this point. First, God will often speak to you through another person. At times, the person whom God selects is someone you would not have picked to bring you the word of the Lord. God's chosen vessel for the moment may very well be someone who really irritates you or has been a thorn in your flesh. In cases like this, your first reaction is to reject the word because you don't like or trust the messenger. However, God will speak to us in situations like this so that we will always remain humble before Him.

Second, God will often speak through negative circumstances. For example, God can use a word that did not originate from Him to speak certain things into our lives. Let me explain. A few years ago I received a "prophetic" word from a person who went to my church at the time. The word was very condemning and judgmental. It brought great discouragement and oppression to my wife and I. Sometime later, without knowing that I had received such a negative word, an internationally respected prophet told me that the word was not from God. He, my wife, and I broke off the curse that this false word had released over us. Immediately, we were free of discouragement and oppression. Interestingly enough, however, though the word did not originate from God, the Lord used it to speak some things to me. He used this negative word to reveal areas that He wanted me to change. Through this traumatic experience, I learned a valuable truth: We should always ask the Lord to speak His words to us in the midst of the entire message. We must all be careful not to reject the message of the Lord because we might tend to reject the messenger.

6. God's voice is not confined to our theological box.

Isaiah 55:8-9 tells us that "God's thoughts are not our thoughts, neither are your ways my ways." Many times, God will speak to us in a way that will be completely different from what we expect. We might be in a certain situation where we have to hear from God. We believe that God will speak to us in a particular way. However, God frequently bypasses our logical conclusions and speaks in an entirely different way than we anticipated.

Earlier, I shared about the time when God told me to have more children. When He spoke those words to me, having more children was not even on my radar screen. My wife and I had no plans to have more children. I was asking God to speak to me within the limits that I had placed on Him. He spoke outside my limits. Often, God will speak in a way that is very different from what we think is the normal or logical way. We must be very careful not to limit the voice of God or to put him into a certain box.

7. God's voice may differ from the opinions of friends or counselors.

Proverbs 11:14 reads, "In abundance of counselors there is victory." Although it is good to seek wise counsel in major decisions, we must be aware that God's voice will often be different, even contradictory, to the advice of friends, pastors and counselors. Even Jesus encountered this. Every reference Jesus made to His disciples about the cross was met with confusion and resistance.

As I think back over my journey with the church I pastor, almost every major decision was met with different voices that were contrary to what God was saying to me. I would sense the leading of the Holy Spirit in one direction, while other people advised me not to go that way. I sensed God's voice telling me one thing while my friends and counselors were telling me another. There were many times I had to stand alone in my decision—knowing that those around me questioned my choice. While I have certainly made mistakes along the way, for the most part, I believe that I have heard God's voice correctly. Be prepared to stand alone when you know you have heard His voice.

8. God's voice should be accompanied by His peace.

Paul said, "Let the peace of God rule in your hearts" (Col. 3:15). For major decisions, I approach the decision-making process from two directions. First, I determine whether or not I have heard from God about the decision. Second, I make sure that I have peace in my heart about my choice. If I am unsure about the answer to either question, I wait on the Lord until I have a stronger sense that I am making the correct decision.

Let me illustrate with an example of something that happened to me a few years ago. Our church was in a close relationship with another church. We did many things together. The senior pastor and I were working in the city together and I was learning much from him. One day, I went to a mountain park near my home to pray. As I was praying, I heard a voice tell me to merge my church with this pastor's church. In one sense, it seemed logical. They had strengths where we were weak, and we had strengths where they were weak. We would also be much larger, which would be helpful in reaching out to more people. But there was one thing nagging at me. I did not have a peace that God was saying this to me. I knew I had heard a voice, and I thought it was God's voice. But the peace of God was not present. So I waited. I held the word in my heart, and I shared it with my wife. We prayed a great deal about this word, but peace never came.

Consequently I never acted on the word. Years later, I realized that the ministry was praying for us to join with them based on their desires and not on the will of God. The voice I heard was the result of their self-centered prayers rather than a word from God. When God speaks, calling us to do significant things, His peace will rule.

Examining How the Voices We Hear Affect Our Lives

In order to discern God's voice from the many voices that we hear, we must examine how the voice affects our lives. God's voice will always produce life while the other voices lead to death. Whether it is the voice of the enemy or the voice of our own souls, the end result will be unfruitful. God's voice will lead us into our destiny whereas other voices will lead us into a dead end. God's voice will guide us along the narrow path that leads to life whereas other voices will lead us down the broad path that leads to destruction. In the last section of this chapter, I want to share three results that a true word from God will produce in our lives. They are listed below. God's voice:

1. Convicts rather than condemns
2. Builds faith, confidence, hope, passion for Jesus and a sense of destiny
3. Produces the fruit of the Spirit

1. God's voice convicts rather than condemns.

For the most part, when God speaks to us, it is to encourage, comfort, and exhort us to go on with Him. However, there are times when God will speak a word of correction to us. When God brings correction, His word convicts whereas the enemy's voice condemns. There are several very important distinctions between the convicting voice of God and the condemning voice of the enemy. These are listed in Table 3.1 on the following page.

True conviction is God's kindness that leads us to repent. Paul told the Roman believers, "The kindness of God leads you to repentance" (Rom. 2:4). When God convicts us, He wants us to change so that we become more like Christ. Conviction is cleansing and refreshing to us. Notice the following Scripture: "Therefore repent and return, so that your sins may be wiped away, in order that times of refreshing may come from the presence of the Lord" (Acts 3:19). When we are convicted and respond by repenting, the action always leads to a refreshing and cleansing feeling in God's presence. On the other hand, condemnation has no power to change us. It only keeps us in the same condition where we feel dirty, discouraged, and defiled. We need to remember that God never condemns us, just like Paul said:

> Therefore there is now no condemnation for those who are in Christ Jesus. For the law of the Spirit of life in Christ Jesus has set you free from the law of sin and of death (Rom. 8:1-2).

Table 3.1: Conviction vs. Condemnation

Conviction	Condemnation
Draws us closer to God	Pushes us away from God
Is specific	Is vague
Restores hope and confidence	Results in discouragement, guilt, and shame
Yields peace, comfort, and life	Yields anxiety, distress, and death
Leads to true repentance and change	Keeps us in the same condition
Makes us feel clean	Makes us feel dirty

2. **God's voice builds faith, confidence, hope, passion for Jesus and a sense of destiny.**

God's voice is life-giving and faith-inspiring. Notice how Jesus speaks to Nathanael:

> Jesus saw Nathanael coming to Him, and said of him, "Behold, an Israelite indeed, in whom is no guile!" Nathanael said to Him, "How do You know me?" Jesus answered and said to him, "Before Philip called you, when you were under the fig tree, I saw you." Nathanael answered Him, "Rabbi, You are the Son of God; You are the King of Israel" (John 1:47-49).

In this passage of Scripture, the Father spoke to Jesus about Nathanael through a vision. In turn, Jesus spoke to Nathanael about what He had seen. He told Nathanael that there was no guile in him. Because of this vision, Nathanael saw Jesus as the Son of God. It resulted in Nathanael following Jesus as a disciple. This brief passage gives us great insight into how God's voice encourages, exhorts, and builds up. Jesus' words to Nathanael instilled faith and hope. It produced the courage and confidence Nathanael needed to follow Jesus. Similarly, in their first encounter, Jesus spoke faith and confidence into the life of Simon when He prophetically called him the Rock (John 1:42).

Another passage of Scripture, 1 Corinthians 14:24-25, adds reinforcement to this concept. It reads:

> But if all prophesy, and an unbeliever or an ungifted man enters, he is convicted by all, he is called to account by all; the secrets of his heart are disclosed; and so he will fall on

his face and worship God, declaring that God is certainly among you.

Many have interpreted this verse of Scripture to imply the exposing of one's sins. Certainly, that is one way to interpret this passage. However, viewing this Scripture from another angle reveals the Heavenly Father's love, care, and detailed attention to a person's life. For example, when a true prophet discloses the details about our lives—information that could not be known by another—it shows that God is truly there, watching over us. Because we feel His love and care for us through the prophetic word, it results in an increased desire to worship and follow Him.

I learned this new perspective from Jeff Burke, a true prophet of God. Jeff ministers at our church from time to time. He possesses a rare gifting in God that allows him to prophesy with great detail and accuracy the secrets of the heart. For the most part, Jeff does not point out the hidden sins of the heart; rather, he discloses the true longings and desires that God has put into His people. After Jeff has ministered, the people he prophesied over know that God is intimately acquainted with them and loves them dearly. They respond with an increased passion for Jesus. Thus, the greatest fruit of Jeff's ministry is a stronger love for God.

God knows our hearts better than we do. He knows our deep secrets and the desires that are locked up within us. When He speaks these secrets to us, it fills us with a deep sense of awe and changes our lives. When God reveals the secrets of our hearts and promises to fulfill our deepest longings, we feel especially loved by the Lord. This strengthens our faith and confidence. It renews our hope and ignites a new passion within us. And it gives us a clearer vision of our destiny.

3. God's voice produces the fruit of the Spirit.
Jesus said that believers would be known by their fruit. The voice of God will produce the fruit of the Spirit in our lives: "Love, joy, peace, patience, kindness, goodness, faithfulness, gentleness, and self control" (Gal. 5:22-23). Let me illustrate. In 2 Corinthians 12:7-10, when God spoke to Paul, it produced great patience and perseverance within him. Jesus told Paul, "My grace is sufficient for you, for power is perfected in weakness." This word resulted in patience—a fruit of the Spirit—in Paul's life. Through this word and the accompanying power that came with it, Paul had grace to be content in all circumstances. He embraced weaknesses, insults, distresses, persecutions, and difficulties for Christ's sake. Hearing God's voice produces inner strength within us. This empowers us to walk in the fruit of the Spirit as we relate to God and others.

THE NARROW PATH OF LIFE

From the time that I began my ministry in 1984, I have seen how important the truths presented in this chapter are. I have seen numerous people shipwrecked in their faith because they did not properly discern the voice of God. I have watched people step out in "faith," thinking they heard God's voice, when they actually heard their own flesh or even worse, the devil.

The path that leads to life is narrow. To walk this path, we must learn to hear the voice of God. At the same time, we must discern God's voice from the voices that we hear. As we learn to decipher God's voice from the others, we must make sure the voices that we hear are consistent with God's character and positively impact our lives.

CHAPTER FOUR

Ministering As Jesus Did

Most assuredly, I say to you, the Son can do nothing of Himself, but what He sees the Father do; for whatever He does, the Son also does in like manner.

JOHN 5:18-20, NKJV

Truly, truly, I say to you, he who believes in Me, the works that I do shall he do also; and greater works than these shall he do; because I go to the Father.

JOHN 14:12

In Chapters 1-2, I discussed the truth that we are called into fellowship with God—to speak to Him and to listen to His voice. Hearing God's voice brings great joy and fulfillment to us. It also allows us to know God's will and destiny for our lives. In these two chapters, I dealt mostly with hearing God's voice for personal edification and direction. In Chapter 3, we saw the importance of discerning God's voice from the other voices that we hear. Chapter 3 applied to hearing God both for personal and ministry purposes. In this chapter, we will make the transition to knowing God's voice for ministry.

This will be our focus for the remainder of the book. Although God speaks to us for reasons other than ministry, if we learn to hear His voice for ministry purposes, we can hear His voice whenever He speaks.

In this chapter, I want to establish the following truth: To be effective in ministry, we must learn to minister like Jesus did. To develop this principle, we will examine Jesus' approach to ministry in more detail and show why this is important to us. By examining the Scriptures, we will see how Jesus heard the voice of God in order to minister effectively. Finally, we will make life application and present the case that we need to minister in the same manner.

Go to the Hospital

Several years ago, when my second son, Michael, was six years old, he played in a children's baseball league. During the season, there was another young boy on his team who was in an automobile accident with his dad. The dad was not hurt, but the young boy had been injured and went into a coma. He had been in the coma for several days when the team heard the news. As you can imagine, all of the parents and the boys were very upset and concerned. Donna and I were really burdened to pray for him and we did, even though we saw no change.

One day I was driving down the interstate highway (I still remember this encounter with God vividly even though it was about 20 years ago). As I was driving, I heard God say to me, "Go to the hospital and pray with the boy." I turned the car immediately toward the hospital and went to the boy's room. He was there in a coma, with his mother by his side. I asked her if I could pray for his recovery. She eagerly gave me permission, even though she and her husband were not Christians. I said a brief prayer and left, seeing no change in the boy's condition. But the next day, I heard the wonderful news: The boy had come out of the coma and had even gone home. God allowed me to be a part of a miracle! Even though the family did not respond positively, I had the opportunity to go visit the family and tell them about Jesus.

From this story, my main point is this: It was essential that I heard God's voice. If I did not hear God tell me to go pray for the boy, I probably would not have gone to the hospital. Instead, I would have just prayed for him from a distance. But God had different plans. He wanted to show His power to this family that did not know Christ. God's voice initiated a supernatural healing that had a huge impact on this family, and on my own life. This example demonstrates a truth that I want to cover in this chapter. In order for us to be effective in ministry, we must imitate the way Jesus ministered. Jesus only did what His Father told Him to do. By obeying the Father's voice, Jesus operated powerfully with great signs, miracles, and wonders.

A Look at How Jesus Ministered

Before we can minister like Jesus did, we must understand how He ministered. There are four key components that characterize how Jesus' ministered. Jesus ministered:

1. In response to the needs of people
2. In response to the voice of the Father
3. In the power of the Holy Spirit

4. After spending much time alone with the Father

1. Jesus ministered in response to the needs of people.
Jesus responded to the requests of the people He encountered. He responded to people's faith. He was moved by compassion when He saw people's needs. Jesus ministered in response to the people around Him. For example, note the following Scripture:

> And it happened when He was in a certain city, that behold, a man who was full of leprosy saw Jesus; and he fell on his face and implored Him, saying, "Lord, if You are willing, You can make me clean." Then He put out His hand and touched him, saying, "I am willing; be cleansed." Immediately the leprosy left him (Luke 5:12-13, NKJV).

2. Jesus ministered in response to the voice of the Father.
Although Jesus ministered in response to the people's needs, His primary method of ministry was based upon His response to the voice of the Father. Note these Scriptures:

> Most assuredly, I say to you, the Son can do nothing of Himself, but what He sees the Father do; for whatever He does, the Son also does in like manner (John 5:18-20, NKJV).

> I can of Myself do nothing. As I hear, I judge; and My judgment is righteous, because I do not seek My own will but the will of the Father who sent Me (John 5:30, NKJV).

Jesus' method of ministry was based upon what He heard

from His Father. He only did what His Father told Him to do. Even when Jesus responded to people's requests, He ministered to them through the wisdom of the Holy Spirit. This is vastly different from the traditional method of ministry that is based mostly upon our response to people's needs or requests.

3. Jesus ministered in the power of the Holy Spirit.

Jesus is God incarnate. He is the unique Son of God, the only begotten of the Father. He is unequalled in character, holiness, power, and purity. He lived a sinless life. He fulfilled the Law with perfect compliance. There has never been another like Him on the earth. Yet, the Bible does not record a single miracle performed by Jesus until the Holy Spirit fell upon Him at His baptism. In fact, after Jesus was baptized, He went into the wilderness full of the Holy Spirit (Luke 4:1) and returned in the power of the Holy Spirit (Luke 4:14). It was after His wilderness testing, when He was filled with the power of God, that He announced the beginning of His ministry. We see this in Luke 4:17-21:

> And the book of the prophet Isaiah was handed to Him. And He opened the book and found the place where it was written, "THE SPIRIT OF THE LORD IS UPON ME, BECAUSE HE ANOINTED ME TO PREACH THE GOSPEL TO THE POOR. HE HAS SENT ME TO PROCLAIM RELEASE TO THE CAPTIVES, AND RECOVERY OF SIGHT TO THE BLIND, TO SET FREE THOSE WHO ARE OPPRESSED, TO PROCLAIM THE FAVORABLE YEAR OF THE LORD." And He closed the book, gave it back to the attendant and

sat down; and the eyes of all in the synagogue were fixed on Him. And He began to say to them, "Today this Scripture has been fulfilled in your hearing."

In an unparalleled way, everything Jesus did was empowered by the Holy Spirit under the direction of the Heavenly Father. He moved in much more power than anyone in history. There is no doubt that His unique nature was a significant reason for this. However, even Jesus needed the anointing of the Holy Spirit to perform great signs, miracles, and mighty deeds. When Jesus returned to the Father He sent the Holy Spirit (John 14:15-30). Just prior to His promise to send us the Spirit, Jesus prophesied that we would walk in even greater power because he was going to the Father. When we are anointed by the Holy Spirit like Jesus was, we can walk in the same power that Jesus did.

4. Jesus ministered after spending much time alone with the Father.

Even though Jesus was anointed with great power, He still had to spend many hours alone in prayer with the Father. Look at Jesus' prayer life in the following Scriptures:

> After He had sent the crowds away, He went up on the mountain by Himself to pray; and when it was evening, He was there alone (Matt. 14:23).

> And it happened that while He was praying alone, the disciples were with Him, and He questioned them, saying, "Who do the people say that I am?" (Luke 9:18).

Then Jesus came with them to a place called Gethsemane, and said to His disciples, "Sit here while I go over there and pray." And He took with Him Peter and the two sons of Zebedee, and began to be grieved and distressed. Then He said to them, "My soul is deeply grieved, to the point of death; remain here and keep watch with Me." And He went a little beyond them, and fell on His face and prayed, saying, "My Father, if it is possible, let this cup pass from Me; yet not as I will, but as You will." And He came to the disciples and found them sleeping, and said to Peter, "So, you men could not keep watch with Me for one hour?" (Matt. 26:36-40).

In the early morning, while it was still dark, Jesus got up, left the house, and went away to a secluded place, and was praying there (Mark 1:35).

After bidding them farewell, He left for the mountain to pray (Mark 6:46).

It was at this time that He went off to the mountain to pray, and He spent the whole night in prayer to God (Luke 6:12).

Jesus knew the secret power of prayer. Prayer was the way He nurtured His relationship with the Father and positioned Him to hear God's voice.

Summarizing Jesus' Pattern of Ministry

Let's summarize the pattern of ministry that Jesus followed. Jesus pursued an intimate relationship with the Father throughout His life on earth. He spent many hours, on a regular basis, in the presence of the Father. He was devoted to prayer, worship, meditating upon the Scriptures, and listening to the Father's voice.

At His baptism, Jesus was anointed for ministry by the Holy Spirit. Through the Holy Spirit's power and because Jesus was unique, He was able to hear clearly the voice of the Father and perform extraordinary miracles. Through the direction of the Father, Jesus ministered deeply into people's lives—healing and delivering them from the works of the devil. As a result of this ministry style, Jesus heard, saw, and knew what the Father was doing and was able to accomplish the Father's work. Jesus' intimate walk with the Father allowed Him to hear the voice of God and obey in the power of the Holy Spirit. We need to minister in the same way.

Examples of Jesus' Pattern of Ministry

Let's take a look at several passages of Scripture that illustrate how Jesus responded to the voice of the Father for ministry. Jesus heard the Father for:

1. Healing the sick
2. Offering salvation to the lost
3. Wisdom to select leadership
4. Wisdom to handle a problem
5. Wisdom to teach
6. Faith for the supernatural

1. **Jesus heard the Father for healing the sick.**

In Luke 5, Jesus miraculously healed a paralyzed man. But notice a very important phrase in Luke 5:17:

> Now it happened on a certain day, as He was teaching, that there were Pharisees and teachers of the law sitting by, who had come out of every town of Galilee, Judea, and Jerusalem. *And the power of the Lord was present to heal them.*

From this passage, we see that the power of God was present for healing on this particular day. Jesus knew that the Father wanted Him to pray for the sick.

In John 5:1-8, Jesus healed a man who was sick for 38 years. What an amazing display of God's power to heal a man that was ill for so long! Yet note verse 6. Jesus asked the man, "Do you wish to get well?" The Father revealed to Jesus the key to this man's healing. It was the desire to be restored. Quite possibly, this man had grown comfortable in his infirmity. He did not have to work. Other people took care of his needs. This man probably had a complacent attitude toward being healed. Because Jesus heard from the Father concerning the root issue, Jesus had the key that would unlock his healing. So before Jesus healed him, he had to stir afresh a desire for healing within him. Once this happened, Jesus instantly restored his ability to walk. Again, we see how hearing God was a necessary part of Jesus' healing ministry.

2. **Jesus heard the Father for offering salvation to the lost.**

John 4 records the powerful encounter of Jesus with the woman at the well. This is probably a familiar story to you. Jesus revealed Himself to the woman and through her salvation, much of the city was saved. A powerful move of God was initiated with that one encounter at the well. Although this is one of the greatest stories of evangelism in the Bible, have you ever thought about how this came about? What caused all of these people to receive Jesus as their Savior? To answer this question, let's look at John 4:39: "And many of the Samaritans of that city believed in Him because of the word of the woman who testified, 'He told me all that I ever did.'" Earlier in the encounter, Jesus heard the voice of the Father. The Father showed Jesus that this woman had been married five times, and she was presently living with a man who was not her husband. Because He heard the Father reveal specific details about her life, it led to her salvation and to the salvation of much of the city.

3. Jesus heard the Father for wisdom to select leadership.

Jesus also heard from the Father about whom to select for leadership. Note this passage from John 1:43-51:

> The following day Jesus wanted to go to Galilee, and He found Philip and said to him, "Follow Me." Now Philip was from Bethsaida, the city of Andrew and Peter. Philip found Nathanael and said to him, "We have found Him of whom Moses in the law, and also the prophets, wrote – Jesus of Nazareth, the son of Joseph." And Nathanael said to him, "Can anything good come out of Nazareth?" Philip said to him, "Come and see." Jesus saw Nathanael coming toward Him, and said of him, "Behold, an Israelite indeed, in whom is no deceit!" Nathanael said to Him, "How do You know me?" Jesus answered and said to him, "Before Philip called you, when you were under the fig tree, I saw you." Nathanael answered and said to Him,

"Rabbi, You are the Son of God! You are the King of Israel!" Jesus answered and said to him, "Because I said to you, 'I saw you under the fig tree,' do you believe? You will see greater things than these." And He said to him, "Most assuredly, I say to you, hereafter you shall see heaven open, and the angels of God ascending and descending upon the Son of Man."

Jesus called Philip to follow Him. Philip then found Nathanael and asked him to follow Jesus. Nathanael had some doubts about following Jesus. These doubts were erased when Jesus told him specific things about his life. Jesus told him that he had seen him under the fig tree even before Philip had called him. He also told him other things about his destiny. Because Jesus received prophetic insight, Nathanael received the courage to be a leader and follow after Jesus. Again, we see powerful results when Jesus obeyed the voice of the Father for ministry.

4. Jesus heard the Father for wisdom to handle a problem.

In John 8, Jesus was thrust into the midst of a real dilemma. The Scribes and Pharisees were trying to put to death a woman caught in adultery. They were also trying to catch Jesus in a violation of the Law in order to accuse Him. His response was amazing. He said "He who is without sin among you, let him be the first to throw a stone at her" (John 8:7). What an answer! What wisdom! Earlier that morning, Jesus had been to the Mount of Olives—most likely to meet with His Father in prayer. As the need arose, He knew from the Father exactly what to say to diffuse a very difficult situation. We see once again how hearing the voice of God helps in ministry situations.

5. Jesus heard the Father for wisdom to teach.

In John 9, Jesus revealed to His disciples that He was the Light of the world. Because of this, He told the disciples that they must do the works of the Father while the opportunity was available. But what led to this teaching opportunity? It was through a blind man's sight being supernaturally restored.

Before Jesus taught about Himself as the Light of the world, He and the disciples saw a blind man. The disciples wanted to know why the man was blind from birth. Jesus told them that it was not due to sin, but so the works of God could be displayed in him. Because Jesus had supernatural wisdom—knowing the reason why the man was afflicted—it led to a miraculous healing and a teaching opportunity. Jesus used this miracle as a picture of what we are like without Him. We walk in spiritual darkness, blinded by sin, until the Light of the world shines into our hearts and guides us into the truth.

6. Jesus heard the Father for faith for the supernatural.

In John 11, Jesus raised Lazarus from the dead. With many people gathered around, it took great faith for Jesus to say "remove the stone" from the tomb. Jesus operated on a level of faith that is far beyond what we are accustomed to. So what gave Jesus the faith to believe that Lazarus would be raised from the dead? Earlier in the chapter, when Lazarus was about to die from his illness, Mary and Martha asked Jesus to heal him. Instead of healing him, Jesus spoke these words of promise: "This sickness is not unto death, but for the glory of God, that the Son of God may be glorified through it" (John 11:4). Jesus heard the voice of the Father speak a promise that He would raise Lazarus from the dead. This word gave Jesus the supernatural faith to perform an extraordinary miracle.

We Need to Minister in the Same Way Jesus Did

Jesus did not minister in the way that He did just because He was the Son of God. Nor was His ministry style applicable to a select few throughout history. Jesus chose this style of ministry for all who followed Him. Note this familiar passage in Mark 3:13-15:

> And He went up on the mountain and called to Him those He Himself wanted. And they came to Him. Then He appointed twelve, that they might be with Him and that He might send them out to preach, and to have power to heal sicknesses and to cast out demons.

Jesus taught the twelve apostles to minister using the following model:

1. Live in an intimate relationship with Him
2. Hear His voice
3. Go out as a sent one, based on His direction, to preach, teach, heal, and cast out demons.

This style of ministry is a model for all believers to follow.

We are all called to minister in the same way Jesus did. As we minister in this style, we will perform great works in His name. Notice what Jesus said about this:

> Truly, truly, I say to you, he who believes in Me, the works that I do shall he do also; and greater works than these shall he do; because I go to the Father (John 14:12).

Jesus said that His disciples would perform greater miracles than He did. Therefore, for us to see this promise fulfilled, we must learn to minister like Jesus did. There are four important reasons why we must learn how to do this. They are listed below. Ministering like Jesus:

1. Bears witness to Him
2. Allows us to do what God is doing
3. Compliments the written Word in accomplishing God's will
4. Builds faith in the person for whom we are praying

1. Ministering like Jesus bears witness to Him.

In John 5:36, Jesus said that His works testified of Him. When we minister as Jesus did, we bear witness to the reality of the Lord Jesus Christ. It also shows the world that the Father sent Him to redeem mankind.

I remember one Sunday morning at church. The father of a lady who attended our church was visiting. He was from another city thousands of miles away, so I had never met him and knew nothing about him. Later, I found out that he was not a Christian. His daughter really wanted him to accept Christ as his Savior. As the service progressed, I began to have difficulty breathing. This feeling only lasted a few seconds, but I knew God was speaking to me about the condition of someone in the room. I asked the Lord what He was saying, and I heard the word "emphysema." At the appropriate time, I asked if there was anyone present who suffered from emphysema. Nobody responded so I went on with the meeting. When the service was over, the lady told me that the word was for her father. God wanted to heal him. But more importantly, God desired the ministry to bear witness to Jesus. This man—whether he responded to the request for prayer or not—knew that God had spoken. The word bore witness to the reality of God to this unsaved man. Had I just asked for anyone with a need to come forward for prayer, it would have had no impact upon the most important issue—that God is real and cares about him.

2. **Ministering like Jesus allows us to do what God is doing.**

Hearing and obeying God allows us to flow in the anointing of the Holy Spirit. Because God is merciful, anytime we minister out of a sincere heart He will bless our prayers and effort. However, God releases far greater power on what He initiates. He will bless what we do, but the greatest anointing comes when we hear His voice and obey.

In recent years, the Lord has allowed me to equip pastors. Whenever I do a pastor's conference, one message that I often teach relates to keeping your worship service in the river of God. I instruct them that God has a specific plan for every meeting. I teach that there is a river that flows from the throne and our task as leaders is to discover the river, jump into it ourselves, and direct the service into it. I tell them that there is life in the river (see Ezek. 47:9) and on the banks of the river, there are trees that produce fruit for food and leaves for healing (see Ezek. 47:12). Hearing God's voice and directing the service accordingly allows us to jump in this river of the Holy Spirit and do what He is doing.

3. **Ministering like Jesus compliments the written Word in accomplishing God's will.**

Many Jewish believers knew about Isaiah's prophecy about the virgin birth. However, Mary did not know that she was the chosen virgin until she heard the voice of God through an angel. Hearing God's voice compliments the written Word by applying it to our lives and ministry situations. For example, we know that God is our healer; however, we often don't know if God wants to heal in a certain service. When we receive a word of knowledge, we know that He desires to heal a certain condition. This builds faith in us and in the person for whom we are praying.

4. **Ministering like Jesus builds faith in the person for whom we are praying.**

When we are ministering to someone and God reveals something to us about them that was previously unknown, it helps them know that God is at work. It helps them know that God is truly speaking, it builds up their faith, and positions them to receive from God.

Think with me about the illustration I shared at the beginning of this chapter. Had I just told the mom that I came to pray for the boy, it would have only produced a certain level of hope. However, when I informed her that God spoke to me and told me to pray for him, it resulted in a level of faith. There is a big difference between hoping for God to move and faith that expects God to move. Hearing God releases faith.

Learn to Minister Like Jesus Did

Every believer has a call to minister. Not everyone will preach or teach, but we are all called to use our gifts to advance the kingdom of God. Ministry is much more fun, rewarding, and powerful if we learn to minister as Jesus did. Maybe you have never seen God move supernaturally as a result of your prayers. Maybe you have only been ministering in response to people's needs. Maybe you have never heard God tell you what He wanted to do. As we conclude this chapter, I want to challenge you to seek God for what He is doing and partner with Him in His work. Learn to minister like Jesus did. Test the results. You will be amazed!

CHAPTER FIVE

HEARING GOD FOR MINISTRY

For to one is given the word of wisdom through the Spirit, and to another the word of knowledge according to the same Spirit; to another faith by the same Spirit, and to another gifts of healing by the one Spirit, and to another the effecting of miracles, and to another prophecy, and to another the distinguishing of spirits, to another various kinds of tongues, and to another the interpretation of tongues.

1 CORINTHIANS 12:7-11

For me, ministering in the gifts of the Holy Spirit is one of the most enjoyable parts of ministry. I love to teach and preach, but being used as a vessel of the Holy Spirit as God moves in supernatural ways is very exciting. A few years ago, when our church was still in a denomination, I attended one of those very boring denominational committee meetings. After we had discussed some administrative issues, God decided to interrupt this meeting and finish it in a dramatic way. God changed a dry committee meeting into one of the most exciting times of my ministry. The Lord spoke and it changed everything.

There were five of us at the meeting. At the end, we decided to join hands for a closing prayer. As another person in the group prayed, I felt a brief, sharp pain in the abdominal area of my body. I wondered for a moment if the pain was a physical discomfort or if God was speaking to me about a ministry opportunity. Occasionally, God speaks to me through feelings in my body, especially when He wants to initiate prayer for healing. I was reluctant to say anything because this group was not accustomed to God speaking in this way. But as I waited for the others to finish praying, I felt increasingly compelled to take a risk and speak out. Finally, I went for it and asked, "Is there someone in the group with abdominal pain?" The lady next to me immediately screamed, "Who is this man?" She of course was speaking of me. She was extremely surprised that someone had perceived her condition without any prior knowledge of it. As it turned out, she was scheduled to have surgery two days later in her abdominal area. The doctors said she had a tumor, quite possibly cancerous, that needed to be removed.

As she shared her story, it was obvious that no one in the group knew what she was facing. After we learned of her need, we gathered around her, laid hands on her and prayed fervently. I called her a few days later to find out the results of her visit to the doctor. She told me her amazing story. As the doctors began to do the surgery, the tumor was gone! Praise God! This was an exciting time for everyone in our group. This dear lady was in complete awe of God because He miraculously healed her. I was overwhelmed with joy because I heard the voice of God and was used to initiate a miracle. And everyone in the group was thrilled because we were allowed to participate in a supernatural work of God.

Through the gifts of the Holy Spirit, a dull committee meeting was transformed into a monumental event. The power of God, as illustrated in this example, is available to everyone. God desires to speak to all of His children in order to initiate, assist, and empower ministry.

An Overview of the Gifts of the Holy Spirit

Hearing God for ministry purposes, which is the theme of this chapter, requires that we learn to function in the gifts of the Holy Spirit. God speaks to us through the gifts to initiate, assist, and empower ministry. Since there is a close connection between hearing God for ministry and operating in the gifts of the Holy Spirit, let's look at the gifts in more detail.

There are several areas in the New Testament where the gifts are mentioned and many references where they are inferred. However, for our study, we will look at the four main passages where Paul taught on the gifts of the Holy Spirit. These passages are listed below:

> And He Himself gave some to be *apostles*, some *prophets*, some *evangelists*, and some *pastors* and *teachers*, for the equipping of the saints for the work of ministry, for the edifying of the body of Christ, till we all come to the unity of the faith and of the knowledge of the Son of God, to a perfect man, to the measure of the stature of the fullness of Christ; that we should no longer be children, tossed to and fro and carried about with every wind of doctrine, by the trickery of men, in the cunning craftiness of deceitful plot-

ting, but, speaking the truth in love, may grow up in all things into Him who is the head—Christ—from whom the whole body, joined and knit together by what every joint supplies, according to the effective working by which every part does its share, causes growth of the body for the edifying of itself in love (Eph. 4:11-16, NKJV).

For just as we have many members in one body and all the members do not have the same function, so we, who are many, are one body in Christ, and individually members one of another. Since we have gifts that differ according to the grace given to us, each of us is to exercise them accordingly: if prophecy, according to the proportion of his faith; if service, in his serving; or he who teaches, in his teaching; or he who exhorts, in his exhortation; he who gives, with liberality; he who leads, with diligence; he who shows mercy, with cheerfulness (Rom. 12:4-8).

And God has appointed in the church, first *apostles*, second *prophets*, third *teachers*, then *miracles*, then gifts of *healings*, *helps*, *administrations*, *various kinds of tongues*. All are not apostles, are they? All are not prophets, are they? All are not teachers, are they? All are not workers of miracles, are they? All do not have gifts of healings, do they? All do not speak with tongues, do they? All do not interpret, do they? (1 Cor. 12:28-30).

But to each one is given the *manifestation of the Spirit* for the common good. For to one is given the *word of wisdom* through the Spirit, and to another the *word of knowledge* according to the same Spirit; to another *faith* by the same

Spirit, and to another gifts of *healing* by the one Spirit, and to another *the effecting of miracles*, and to another *prophecy*, and to another *the distinguishing of spirits*, to another *various kinds of tongues*, and to another the *interpretation of tongues*. But one and the same Spirit works all these things, distributing to each one individually just as He wills (1 Cor. 12:7-11).

Recently, there have been many teachings and writings about the gifts. From these numerous sources, a variety of categorizations have emerged. Let's follow down this path and organize the gifts. This will help us understand the gifts of the Spirit better.

From Ephesians 4:11-16, we have the Fivefold Leadership Gifts. These gifts identify the types of ministry leaders that are called to equip the Body of Christ for effective service. Romans 12:4-8 lists the Ministry Gifts. Some people refer to these as Motivational Gifts. Although they do identify our motivation for ministry, they also express an aspect of a person's ministry calling. The gifts listed in 1 Corinthians 12:7-11 are the Manifestations of the Spirit. Whereas the first two listings are more permanent in nature, the manifestation gifts are distributed to all as a ministry need arises. Therefore, these gifts are more temporary in nature. In 1 Corinthians 12:28-30, Paul presents a fourth listing; however, this reference does not identify new gifts that are not identified elsewhere. Instead, his main point is to explain the different gifts in the Body of Christ and how everyone will function in a unique way. The definitions and Table 5.1 on the following page summarize what we have talked about so far in this section.

- Fivefold Leadership Gifts: Ministry leaders that are called to equip the Body of Christ for effective service.

- Ministry Gifts: God-given abilities that express our motivation and calling in ministry.

- Manifestations of the Holy Spirit: Temporary demonstrations of the Holy Spirit's power in order to meet a specific need at a given moment.

Table 5.1: The Gifts of the Holy Spirit Listed and Categorized

Fivefold Leadership Gifts	Ministry Gifts	Manifestations of the Holy Spirit
1. Apostle	1. Prophecy	1. Word of wisdom
2. Prophet	2. Service	2. Word of knowledge
3. Evangelist	3. Teaching	3. Faith
4. Pastor	4. Exhortation	4. Gifts of healing
5. Teacher	5. Giving	5. Effecting of miracles
	6. Leading	6. Prophecy
	7. Mercy	7. Distinguishing of spirits
		8. Various kinds of tongues
		9. Interpretation of tongues

To operate properly in any of the gifts listed above, we must know God's voice. For example, to be an effective giver, we need to hear God tell us who to give to and how much we should give. To function as a prophet, we need to hear God's voice for the prophetic word. To be a competent leader, we need to hear God for the vision into which to lead the people. However, for the purposes of this book, we will focus on the third category of gifts—the manifestations of the Holy Spirit from 1 Corinthians 12:7-11.

An Overview of the Nine Manifestations of the Holy Spirit

To grow in ministry effectiveness, it is imperative that we place a high priority on the gifts of the Holy Spirit listed in 1 Corinthians 12:7-11. Jesus ministered in this fashion. Sometimes He would receive a word of knowledge or word of wisdom. Other times He would give a prophetic word or perform a miracle. We need to function in the gifts just like Jesus did. To do this, we need to practice and utilize these gifts.

The nine manifestations of the Holy Spirit are not permanent gifts. Instead, they are tools given to empower effective ministry as the need arises. They are given for the common good of the body according to the will of the Lord. At any given time, each of us can function in any of the nine gifts.

Over the years, this issue has created considerable confusion. Many people believe they only have one or two of these gifts. Some think that one person may be gifted only in the word of knowledge or in the word of wisdom. Or that certain individuals only function in the ability to distinguish spirits.

This is an incorrect way to interpret this passage of Scripture. Instead, a better way to look at these gifts is to expect that every person can operate in all nine gifts. Each of us can and should experience all nine of these gifts as the Holy Spirit determines we have need of them. Since a believer has access to all nine manifestations of the Holy Spirit, we can minister just like Jesus did.

Describing the Nine Manifestations of the Holy Spirit

Now that we have seen an overview of the nine gifts of the Holy Spirit, I want to define and illustrate these gifts in a practical way. This will help us understand the different ways in which the Holy Spirit might use us in ministry. The nine manifestations of the Holy Spirit are:

1. Words of knowledge
2. Words of wisdom
3. Distinguishing of spirits
4. Faith
5. Healing
6. Miracles
7. Prophecy
8. Tongues
9. Interpretation of tongues

1. Words of knowledge

Definition: A revelation of information for a person,

group, or situation that could not have been known by natural means.

Illustration: The story that I told at the beginning of this chapter illustrates a word of knowledge. I had no prior information about the lady's abdominal condition. Yet God knew and He opened up heaven just for a moment to give me specific insight into her condition. This revelation led to her healing. Through a word of knowledge, great blessing came to this lady because she was healed, to me because I was used to initiate a miracle, and to the entire group because we were used to administer healing through the power of the Holy Spirit.

2. **Words of wisdom**

Definition: A revelation of supernatural wisdom that enables a person to know what to do or say in a particular circumstance.

Illustration: The story that I told at the beginning of Chapter 4 about the young boy in the coma illustrates a word of wisdom. In this case, I knew the boy was in a coma. I knew which hospital he was in. I didn't need supernatural knowledge for this. What I needed was the wisdom of God to know how to minister to him. I needed the wisdom to know that I was to go pray with him rather than just for him. The result was a mighty healing and an exciting testimony. If I had not heard God through a word of wisdom, I would not have gone to pray with the boy. God may have chosen to heal him anyway, but I would have missed out on a wonderful blessing.

3. **Distinguishing of spirits**

Definition: The ability to discern what type of spirit is in operation in a given situation.

Illustration: Since 1992, the Lord has used my wife and I to minister deliverance. During this time, we have had the joy of ministering to hundreds of people in this way. Although this gift is used in other ways, distinguishing or discerning of spirits is essential for an effective deliverance ministry. People come for ministry with symptoms, but they don't always know the root cause of the problem. Many times they are not aware of the entry point that gave access to the specific demonic spirit or spirits they are dealing with. As God communicates to us through this gift, He reveals the specific spirit that is operating. By knowing this, we can deal with the appropriate spirit.

I remember the first time I actually cast out a demon. Though I had seen others do it, I never had an opportunity to do it myself. One Sunday morning after I had preached a message on the power of the blood of Jesus, I sensed the Lord giving me a word to initiate ministry. I heard in my spirit the phrase "spirit of addiction." I called for everyone who struggled with a spirit of addiction to come forward for prayer. Three people came forward that morning. One lady came who was addicted to cigarettes. She wanted to stop but couldn't. As I began to pray for her, I noticed her hands stiffen and contort in an unusual way. I knew immediately that a demon was manifesting. It took a while, but by the power of the blood of Jesus and the ministry of the Holy Spirit, we cast the demon out. This was an exciting day for our church and for this lady who was set free from cigarette addiction. It all began with the gift of distinguishing of spirits.

4. **Faith**

Definition: An unexplainable impartation of assurance that God will act on our behalf.

Illustration: In 1983, I had my own business and was trying to sell it in order to go into ministry. We were having major problems selling the company, and I had given up hope. I believed we were headed for serious financial collapse. On the other hand, my wife had heard from God. The Lord gave her a word that imparted supernatural faith that our company would sell. To make a long story short, we both held on to the word, believing that it was from God. Finally, after painfully waiting for God's word to be fulfilled, to His glory and our great benefit, the sale went through. This enabled us to launch out into full-time ministry.

5. **Healing**

Definition: The immediate or gradual restoration of health to the body, mind or emotions through the power of the Holy Spirit.

Illustration: Although I have already given several examples of healing throughout the book, I want to highlight two important components of the gifts of healing. First, healing can be instantaneous or it can come as a gradual process that requires repeated prayer for breakthrough. Second, there is not just a gift of healing—there are gifts of healing. The Holy Spirit gives many different types of healing gifts to His people. Some people may have a greater anointing for healing cancer. Others might be more effective in healing back pain or heart problems.

6. **Miracles**

Definition: A supernatural demonstration of God's power that bypasses the natural laws and transforms nature, circumstances, or individual needs.

Illustration: In 1995, my wife and I went to the hospital to pray for one of our church members' relatives. I remember the day vividly. It was a very rainy, cold day. I really didn't want to go, and I didn't expect much to happen. The lady that we were praying for was struggling with congestive heart failure. She was an elderly lady and many did not think she would survive. The medicine the doctors gave her created problems with her kidneys. She had been in a difficult place for several days. The doctors and family were losing hope, and prayer seemed to be the only answer for her. As my wife and I began to pray, we felt the anointing fall upon our prayers. Our faith level increased immediately, and we began to pray more boldly. After a few minutes of prayer, we left with no apparent change in her condition. But within a few hours, her condition improved dramatically. She went home within a day or so. The miraculous part about this story is the heavenly encounter that she experienced that day. Shortly after we left the room, she told her family that a man dressed totally in white clothing entered the room and touched her chest. After he touched her, she knew she was healed. Since several of her family members were not believers, God revealed to them His miracle-working power. Praise God!

7. **Prophecy**

Definition: Speaking forth the mind and counsel of God to edify, exhort, comfort, warn or direct.

Illustration: When I first started our church, I received a prophetic word that was a tremendous encouragement. The word pertained to our church and me. It was a word that revealed God's purpose and destiny for us. It also gave me the wisdom to deal with some serious problems that I faced as the years went on. Through this word, the Lord said that some major problems would arise, but if I would trust Him, He would carry me through. This comforted me when the problems began to surface. I knew that if I simply trusted the Lord that He would help me and bring me through in victory. The word is far too lengthy to present here. However, without this word, I am convinced that I would not have made it to this point in my ministry. Through this prophetic word, I was helped, encouraged, comforted, and warned. This word empowered me to persevere until the Lord brought breakthrough.

8. Tongues

Definition: A form of spiritual communication with God that originates in our spirit, is controlled by our will, is directed by the Holy Spirit, is normally unknown to the speaker, and leads to our edification.

Illustration: The gift of tongues can be exercised personally or corporately. When we pray in tongues individually, our spirit is strengthened and built up. It also causes our faith to grow stronger. This is an invaluable tool for the individual believer.

When the gift of tongues is practiced in a corporate setting, an interpretation must follow. When this happens, tongues and prophecy are equal in importance. Although it seems that in many places the public expression of tongues has been replaced by corporate prophecy, our experience has been to not ignore this important gift. At times, when the Lord is trying to get our attention in a serious way, He will release the gift of tongues. When this gift is expressed, it gets everyone's attention and they are ready to hear the interpretation. In Chapter 8, we will look at the gift of tongues in much more detail.

9. Interpretation of tongues

Definition: The supernatural ability to translate and express the content of what has been spoken through the gift of tongues.

Illustration: There are two main ways that an interpretation to a tongues message comes. Most commonly, the tongues message is given and the interpretation follows. The actual tongues message serves as a catalyst for the interpretation. In other words, it stirs the heart of the interpreter and the translation of the tongues message is given much like a prophetic word. Less frequently, the interpretation comes word-for-word as the tongues message is delivered.

I have given an interpretation to a tongues message on several occasions. Normally, while a person is speaking in tongues, I will receive a phrase in my spirit and as I speak it, I receive more. I remember one time our worship leader was singing in tongues. It was very beautiful and a sense of God's presence filled the room. As she was singing, I began to get the interpretation word-for-word. It was so exciting. As I looked and listened to her, I understood every word she was singing.

Becoming Alert to Our Spiritual Senses

In a moment, we will talk about the different ways that God communicates to us through the gifts of the Holy Spirit. However, before we get into the specifics, I want to mention briefly how we relate to God through our spiritual senses. All of us know that we interact with the outside world through our natural senses. We have senses of sight, sound, touch, taste, and smell. In the same way that we have natural senses, we also have spiritual senses. Through our spiritual senses we relate to God. For example, we can hear God's voice; see in the Spirit; or feel in the Spirit. Although some people have said that they can smell in the Spirit or taste in the Spirit, our experience has been that most people either hear, see, or feel in the Spirit. None of these senses is better than any other.

I remember when I first understood that I could receive communication from God. I really wanted to see visions. I would get jealous of others who received great visions from God. I even got angry with the Lord because He didn't speak to me in that way. For several years, it was a real source of frustration for me. Gradually, I began to realize that I was created to hear and feel in the Spirit rather than see in the Spirit. Finally, when I accepted that the way God speaks to me was not inferior to the way He speaks to others, I had tremendous peace. From that time onward, I became confident in my own ability to hear from God. Through this, I placed a greater importance on what God said rather than how God said it. The main purpose of our spiritual senses is to receive communication from God in order to accomplish His will.

In order to recognize God's communication to us through our spiritual senses, we must be spiritually alert. We need to be in tune with our spirit-man—always aware of our spiritual senses. This is a major factor in discerning that God is speaking to our spirit. I believe that God speaks regularly to many people who do not recognize His voice. They have not yet perceived that the things they feel, see, hear or know is actually God's voice to them! When people awake to these promptings of the Spirit, they begin to move in the gifts in powerful ways.

How God Communicates to Us through the Hearing Gifts

Now that we have a foundational understanding of the nine gifts of the Spirit and of our need to be alert to our spiritual senses, let's focus on how God communicates to us through the gifts. This communication requires an understanding of how the gifts operate through revelation, through speaking, and through power. The definitions and Table 5.2 will help us grasp this truth.

- Revelation Gifts: The gifts of the Holy Spirit that communicate unknown information to us.

- Speaking Gifts: The gifts of the Holy Spirit that are expressed through speaking.

- Power Gifts: The gifts of the Holy Spirit that activate and release God's power.

Table 5.2: The Revelation, Speaking, and Power Gifts

Revelation Gifts	Speaking Gifts	Power Gifts
1. Word of wisdom	1. Prophecy	1. Faith
2. Word of knowledge	2. Various kinds of tongues	2. Gifts of healing
3. Distinguishing of spirits	3. Interpretation of tongues	3. Effecting of miracles

In actuality, five of these nine gifts involve recognizing God's voice and then speaking or acting upon what God has said. These five gifts can be further classified as Hearing Gifts. They are:

1. Words of knowledge
2. Words of wisdom
3. Distinguishing of spirits
4. Prophecy
5. Interpretation of tongues

One important key to functioning in any of the manifestations of the Holy Spirit is to recognize the voice of God through one of these Hearing Gifts. In this section, we will look at how God communicates to us through the Hearing Gifts. In other words, we will see common ways that God may give us a word of knowledge, a word of wisdom or a prophecy. We are focusing on common communication channels that God uses to transmit information to us. Although there are many ways that we may hear from God, we will not try to present every one. Instead, we will look at nine common ways that God speaks to us through the gifts of the Spirit. We should expect regular communication from God to us in one or more of these nine ways:

1. Internal audible voice
2. A phrase
3. A word
4. A rhema word
5. Supernatural intuition
6. Feelings in the body

7. Sensing someone else's burden or bondage
8. Dreams
9. Visions

1. Internal Audible Voice

When God speaks through an internal audible voice, we hear an actual voice in our spirit-man. It is internal and not heard by others. However, it appears as though someone were speaking to us within our inner man.

As I review my walk with the Lord, I can remember two occasions when I heard God speak to me in this way. The impression came somewhat like a strong thought, but it was louder and clearer within my spirit. In both cases, there was absolutely no doubt that God was speaking to me. I didn't wonder if this was God or if I was imagining it. I knew it was God. In both cases, I was in tremendous turmoil over issues that were affecting the church that I pastor. I needed an answer. Once God spoke clearly to me, I knew how to handle the situations and peace entered my heart.

2. A Phrase

Most often, when we hear God speak to us through a phrase, it is more of a thought than an internal voice. Frequently, it is just the beginning of what God desires to speak. As we act on the phrase, we usually receive additional revelation. Often, prophetic words begin with a small phrase.

Many times, when God is giving me a prophetic word either for an individual or a group, He will only give me a fragment of a sentence. As I begin to speak the prophetic word based upon this, more revelation comes. Often the sentence fragment will be what primes the pump. As you speak out in faith, you become a conduit for the Lord to speak through you. Most of what you say bypasses your mind and comes directly from your spirit to your voice. Words of knowledge, words of wisdom and discernment can also come as a phrase.

3. A Word

A word comes just as it sounds. In our thoughts, we may hear one word. For example, when ministering in deliverance, the Holy Spirit will give us discerning of spirits. We then hear one word—the name of the demonic spirit that we need to address to liberate a person from bondage. In praying for the sick as well, we may hear a word like *heart*. This word is intended to give us insight into how we should minister. This word implies that there are some people present that need prayer for their hearts. From my experience, it seems as if God speaks a "word" most often as words of knowledge, words of wisdom or discerning of spirits.

4. The Rhema Word

Rhema is actually the Greek transliteration meaning *utterance or spoken word*. One application of rhema—which is important in hearing the voice of God—is when a word of Scripture is quickened in our spirit as a now word for a particular situation. Let me illustrate with an example from my own life. Recently, I have been praying that God would use our ministry training center, Life School International (LSI), to prepare the nations for the return of the Lord (see the back of the book for more information on LSI). At the same time, I have been seeing the number "222" everywhere. After repeatedly seeing this number on clocks, signs, and license plates, I knew that God was trying to speak to me. At first I did not understand what He was saying. However, one day I came across 2 Timothy 2:2 and it stuck in my spirit. Finally, I realized that God was giving me this verse as a "rhema" word for LSI. In 2 Timothy 2:2, Paul instructs us to entrust our teachings with faithful men and women who can in turn teach others. Through this "rhema" word, the Lord was giving me a strategy of multiplication to spread LSI throughout the world. Ever since the Lord gave me this word, I have been praying with God's strategy and wisdom for LSI. I have been asking God to give me faithful people in the nations that we can teach who will also be able to teach others.

5. Supernatural Intuition

Supernatural intuition is when we have immediate knowledge about God's will without conscious reasoning. In other words, we just know the will of God in a particular circumstance. Although we don't hear a specific word or phrase in our spirit, we intuitively know what is happening in a situation, and we know what God wants us to do. It is important to understand that this type of knowing is spiritual. It is not the same as knowing something in our mind or feeling something in our emotions. It is a knowing in our spirit-man.

Frequently, God speaks to me through supernatural intuition, especially when I need wisdom. As a pastor, I constantly need God's wisdom to guide me and help me make decisions. I need more than human wisdom that is based on facts, data, and reasoning. I need supernatural wisdom from God. When God gives me His wisdom, I just know what needs to be done. In my spirit, I am unmistakably clear about what God is saying. Although I haven't heard anything in particular, I just know. Don't underestimate this way of God speaking. It may not be as glamorous as getting a vision or a dream, but it is a very important way to hear God.

6. Feelings in the Body

Many times during ministry, God speaks to me through a temporary pain or discomfort in my body. This awakens me to the area in which the Lord desires to bring healing. For example, if the Lord wants you to pray for heart problems, He may give you a brief pain in your chest area. If He wants you to pray for asthma, He may give you a temporary shortness of breath. If He wants to minister to knees, He may give you a pain in your knee. Often, He will combine the feeling in the body with a word. Very often, feelings like this are used as words of knowledge to initiate healing.

A few years ago, I was ministering at a church in Fiji. Even though the meeting was going quite well, I knew that the power of God had not yet been released. I was speaking about God's special love for the people at this church. As I finished my message on God's love, I had a sharp, momentary pain in my chest. Immediately, I heard the word "heart" in my spirit. Because the pain was so sharp, I knew that there were some people with serious heart problems.

I invited everyone with heart problems to come forward for prayer. Though I was expecting only one or two people, to my surprise, at least thirty came forward. In addition, the Lord spoke to me about those who were hurting in their heart because they did not really know the love of God. As we began to pray for these people, the power of God came into the meeting. God moved in a very special way. He liberated many people by revealing His love to them. This wonderful demonstration of God's power was initiated by a feeling in my body!

7. Sensing Someone Else's Burden or Bondage

At times, the Lord will allow you to temporarily feel the burden or bondage that someone else is experiencing. You may feel depressed, frustrated, overwhelmed, hopeless or any number of other emotions. When you experience these emotions, and nothing has happened to make you feel this way, you might be hearing from God. The Lord could be giving you a revelation of what someone else feels. Because God allows you to encounter these feelings, He is showing you what another person is experiencing. These emotions—or feelings—come so you can pray for people or minister to them.

In a similar way, you can feel in your spirit the bondage that someone else experiences. You may walk into a room and sense lust or witchcraft. You may meet or pass by someone and feel anger, frustration or just sense that something is wrong in the person's life. You could very well be experiencing what they are going through. Please note that these feelings should be temporary. The Lord gives us this insight so that we will know how to pray or minister to a particular person. Remember: Jesus took man's burdens to the cross. We do not have to take on another's depression, anger, or hopelessness to free them. Jesus already did this. We feel these emotions temporarily in order to help lead them to victory and freedom.

God often speaks to my wife in this way. Sometimes, when she walks into a room, she will experience what someone is feeling. At other times, she can go into a city or region and feel the territorial spirits that are over that area. She doesn't have to stay under these bondages or burdens but receives them only to know how to pray or minister.

A good example to illustrate this way of hearing God comes to mind. A group from our church went to a conference in downtown Atlanta. After the conference, one of the ladies who attended told us this story. As the speaker was ministering, she began to feel lustful thoughts toward him. For her to think this way about anyone was totally unlike her. As her mind wandered, she was very surprised that she was having these struggles and she asked the Lord the reason for them. The Lord told her it was because of the other friend who went to the conference with us. This friend was having some marriage problems and had been flirting with a man from the office where she worked. The lady from our church picked up the issue that was going on with her friend.

8. Dreams

Many times God will speak in dreams. Not all dreams are from God, but often He will give us a dream to provide insight, knowledge or wisdom about an issue. Quite a few books have been written about dreams and how to interpret them. For example, certain animals and objects can have specific meanings that help in their interpretation. However, the ultimate interpretation comes by seeking the Lord diligently. Since dreams are somewhat of a parable, we must rely on the Lord to help us decode them. As we inquire of the Lord about a dream's meaning, He will show us.

Dreams can be a powerful way to hear from God. God may use a dream to speak to us in areas that we would not even consider. Since our mind is idle, He bypasses our preconceived ideas or limits. Michael, my second son, has a lot of dreams. Many of these are helpful in dealing with ministry issues. Others give alerts to prayer needs in the city or nation. Some are even warnings that awaken us to potential difficulties. Dreams are a most helpful way that God speaks to His people.

9. Visions

A vision is a picture within our spirit-man that occurs while we are awake. A vision can be in color or black and white. It can be a brief picture that appears in our mind or it can be extensive. We can have a vision while our eyes are open or shut. A vision is intended to help us see things in the spirit. Many times, a vision requires interpretation. This requires that we hear from God about how to translate the intended meaning. Visions are very powerful in ministry situations. As the saying goes, "A picture is worth a thousand words." A vision adds vivid insight that far surpasses the limitations of words.

The wife of an Elder in our church has visions quite often. When we are ministering to people, I generally ask her to be a part of our ministry team. Her visions add so much insight into the needs of the person we are praying for. It is great when you can have a team of people praying and ministering together. One team member might have a vision while another might hear a word or feel in the spirit. When a team functions together—each knowing God's voice in the different ways that He speaks—the person you are ministering to receives a blessing.

My Journey of Learning to Hear God's Voice

As I wrote this chapter, I thought back on my journey into experiencing the gifts of the Holy Spirit. I have been on this venture since 1983. Through the years, my ability to hear God's voice through the gifts has grown and matured. What began as a small seed has grown into a fruit bearing tree.

As I recall my own experiences, I have operated in all nine of the gifts and have heard from the Lord in the nine common ways that He speaks. For me, it began with the word of wisdom, the word of knowledge, and gifts of healing. Later, I began to function in prophecy and distinguishing of spirits. As ministry opportunities expanded, I experienced the gifts of faith, miracles, tongues, and the interpretation of tongues. I still experience particular gifts more than others. I tend to operate in prophecy, words of knowledge, words of wisdom, and distinguishing of spirits more than the power gifts of healing, faith, and miracles. I still hear and feel in the Spirit more often than I have visions or dreams. Though this is true, I still desire to minister in all nine of the gifts more frequently and to hear the Lord more often in the nine common ways that He speaks.

Hearing God's voice has added tremendous excitement and blessing to my walk with the Lord. It has also blessed many people that I have ministered to over the years. I encourage you to begin or continue your journey into recognizing God's voice for ministry. I can assure you: It will be exciting!

CHAPTER SIX

KEYS TO HEARING GOD'S VOICE

And He did not do many miracles there because of their unbelief.

MATTHEW 13:58

Pursue love, yet earnestly desire spiritual gifts, but especially that you may prophesy.

1 CORINTHIANS 14:1

In this chapter, we will look at six basic principles that will help us hear the voice of God more effectively. These six principles are keys that help us grow in the ability to recognize God's voice. They are also disciplines that we must practice on a regular basis. In every area of the Christian life, we are encouraged to grow in certain skills and disciplines. For example, we must grow in the knowledge of the Word. We must grow in our abilities to teach, to pray or to share the gospel. When we are born-again, we are immature and therefore must develop into seasoned disciples. We must mature in every discipline of the Christian faith. Hearing God's voice is no exception. We must sharpen our skills in hearing God's voice and apply what we hear just as much as a teacher, pastor, or evangelist develops in their areas of gifting. This chapter will help us become proficient in hearing and discerning God's voice. I encourage you to really heed these principles so that you can become skilled at operating in the gifts of the Holy Spirit.[1]

KEY # 1: A LIFESTYLE OF REGULAR TIME IN THE PRESENCE OF THE LORD

Since I discussed this concept extensively in Chapter 2, I won't say too much more about it now. The main reason that I repeat it here is to emphasize the important connection between spending time in God's presence and hearing His voice. As I said in Chapter 2, intimacy with the Lord strengthens our spirit-man. Each of us has spiritual senses that enable us to discern in the spirit realm. However, our spirit-man must be sensitized by the Holy Spirit for this to happen. For example, a musician is trained to hear notes and melodies by playing and listening to music. A hunter must train his eyes to see deer and wild life by being in the woods. In the same way, we train our spiritual senses by spending time in the presence of God.

Private times in the presence of God are the primary training ground for growing and developing our spiritual senses. The disciplines of private worship, personal prayer, Bible study, and meditation upon the words of Scripture heighten our spiritual senses and cause us to be more aware of God's voice.

We should not come into the presence of God just to get something. Often, we come to God because we have a problem that needs to be fixed, or we want God to do something for us. Many times, we come to God in order to get whereas God desires a relationship with us. Jesus speaks about this in John 15:14-16:

> No longer do I call you slaves, for the slave does not know what his master is doing; but I have called you friends, for all things that I have heard from My Father I have made known to you.

Those that are the closest to God will hear His voice most often. As we develop a friendship with God and desire to be in His presence just because we love Him, we will hear His voice with greater frequency and clarity.

Key # 2: Belief and Expectancy

Belief and expectancy are essential ingredients to hearing the voice of God and moving in the gifts of the Holy Spirit. We will only hear God to the degree that we believe and expect Him to speak to us. Often, a person must overcome certain strongholds of unbelief and fear in order to hear the voice of God. Unbelief usually originates from religion, tradition, or a ritualistic church background that might have been ingrained in us. Fear can originate from an unhealthy anxiety that we might miss God, say the wrong thing, or be rejected by people whom we respect and admire. When I help people learn to hear the voice of God, almost everyone has to overcome some form of unbelief and fear. Conquering these mindsets is essential to developing an ongoing ability to hear God. Victory over these destructive thinking patterns increases as we develop belief and expectancy. For the purposes of this book, I have defined belief and expectancy below:

- Belief: A heart attitude that acknowledges God's ability and desire to speak to His people regularly. It is an attitude that accepts the truth that God still communicates to us through the gifts of the Holy Spirit.

- Expectancy: A heart attitude that anticipates and waits for God to speak to us as individuals. It is a mindset that inspires us to linger in God's presence until we hear His voice.

Belief and expectancy are very similar mindsets. They are partner attitudes that work together to enable us to hear from God. Although they are quite similar, there are some key differences. Belief expects God to speak in general to His people. Belief is rooted in the doctrinal truth that God still speaks, and that the gifts of the Spirit are for today. On the other hand, expectancy is a personal desire and anticipation that God will speak to me; such expectancy is accompanied by an eager waiting in His presence until I hear His voice. With these working definitions in mind, let's look at belief and expectancy in more detail.

Belief

To give us confidence that God still speaks and that we can hear His voice, let's look at three important aspects of belief. These three characteristics might identify mindsets in us that need correcting if we want to hear God's voice. They are:

1. In our lives, God is only as big as we believe Him to be.
2. We must believe in the reality of the gifts.
3. We must believe in the importance of the gifts.

1. In our lives, God is only as big as we believe Him to be.

The Bible teaches that if we believe, we can move mountains. Note Mark 11:22-24:

> And Jesus answered saying to them, "Have faith in God. Truly I say to you, whoever says to this mountain, 'Be taken up and cast into the sea,' and does not doubt in his heart, but believes that what he says is going to happen, it will be granted him. Therefore I say to you, all things for which you pray and ask, believe that you have received them, and they will be granted you."

However, if we don't believe, we put a constraint upon God. Note Matthew 13:57-58:

> And they took offense at Him. But Jesus said to them, "A prophet is not without honor except in his hometown and in his own household." And He did not do many miracles there because of their unbelief.

If I believe that God will meet my financial needs, He will. If I believe that He will protect me, He will. If I believe that He will speak to me, I will hear His voice. For many people, hearing the voice of God through a word, dream, or vision is totally outside their belief system. People who have this mentality will rarely hear the voice of God through the gifts of the

Spirit. The first step in hearing God's voice is to believe that He will speak to us regularly in the ways discussed in this book. A clear principle of Scripture is that God will only move in or through your life to the extent that you believe. In your life, He will only be as big as you believe Him to be.

2. We must believe in the reality of the gifts.

In America, much of the Church believes that the gifts of the Holy Spirit are not for today. The Church has embraced a belief system rooted in the cessation of the gifts. The teaching goes like this: Once the last Apostle died and the Scriptures were finalized, there was no need for the gifts of the Holy Spirit. Gifts such as prophecy, tongues, discerning of spirits, words of knowledge, and words of wisdom are deemed irrelevant, unnecessary and even dangerous. Many church leaders teach that the pattern of ministry recorded in the Book of Acts was only needed during the early years of the Church.

Growing up, I went to a church that did not believe in the gifts. This church taught us that God only spoke through the written Word. Since there were sixty-six books of the Bible, that was enough. We did not need to hear God's voice for fellowship or direction. I was taught that God no longer moved through gifts of the Holy Spirit.

In my journey of learning to hear God's voice, I had to overcome mindsets of unbelief that were instilled within me. I came to realize that God actually desired to speak to me. Through studying the Scriptures, I also saw that the gifts never passed away, and that they were still available to the modern Church. For the most part, people with this same attitude will not hear God outside of the written Word and will not be used in the gifts of the Holy Spirit. For us to grow spiritually as people who hear God's voice and are used in power ministry, we must be willing to lay down our denominational teachings and traditions and accept the truth that the gifts are for today.

3. We must believe in the importance of the gifts.

While many others in the American Church believe that the gifts are for today, they do not view the gifts as an essential component for effective ministry. These people view the gifts as irrelevant for the modern Church.

When I served as an associate minister in a specific denominational church, most of the people had this mindset. It was a great church and the pastor was a powerful man of God who moved in the gifts. However, most of the people thought the gifts were great for other countries, but unnecessary in America. The mentality that existed in this church is indicative of many committed Christians in America. They believe that the gifts are for today, but they view them as irrelevant for effective ministry.

Thus, to hear God's voice and move in the gifts of the Holy Spirit, we must overcome both of these beliefs. We must know that the gifts of the Spirit are relevant for today and that they are important for effective ministry.

Expectancy

It is not enough to merely recognize the importance of God still speaking today, but we also must expect God to speak to us. As stated earlier, expectancy and belief are somewhat different. Expectancy is a heart attitude that anticipates and waits for God to speak to us personally. We have just seen the role that belief plays in hearing from God. Our level of belief must not limit God and we must believe in the importance of God speaking today. While belief is a mindset that God still speaks in general, expectancy personalizes our faith so that we wait on God's voice ourselves. Let's look now at three aspects of expectancy. They are:

1. I must expect God to speak to me.
2. I must expect God to speak through me into the lives of others.
3. I must be willing to step out of my comfort zone.

1. I must expect God to speak to me.

Many Christians only believe that God will speak to pastors, prophets, evangelists, and other "special people." However, to hear from the Lord, I must expect God to speak to me. Therefore, expectancy requires that I personalize my faith. By doing this, I not only believe that God will speak to others, I am confident that God will speak to me.

I remember my own journey of learning to hear the voice of God. I was very eager to hear the Lord in order to operate effectively in ministry. On many occasions, I went to meetings where an anointed man or woman of God ministered. They would share a word of knowledge that produced powerful results. Or they would deliver a prophetic word that would really bless someone. During this time, I recall how I longed to prophesy or share a word of knowledge like these people. I longed to minister like them. Although I believed that God moved like this today, I did not expect Him to use me. I had belief, but no expectancy. Finally, I reached a point when I would say to myself, "I can do that." It was not until I reached this level of confident expectation that I began to hear God's voice for ministry. Expecting God to speak to us personally is a much more difficult step of faith than a general belief that God still speaks today. However, to hear and minister in the gifts of the Holy Spirit, it is necessary.

2. I must expect God to speak through me into the lives of others.

Another component of expectancy is having confidence that God will use me to minister into the lives of others. I must expect to hear God on behalf of others and then speak to them what I have heard. At this point, we might battle fear and uncertainty. Questions flood our minds, such as, "Who am I to hear like this?", "Did I really hear God?", "Is this word correct?", or "What if I say this and it is completely wrong?" As we determine to minister into the lives of others, these questions are very common.

We must overcome these feelings of timidity in order to share with others what God has spoken to us. To do this, we must come to the point of trusting God completely. We must know that God is trustworthy and faithful. As we lean on God, knowing that He will not let us down, He will come through for us!

3. I must be willing to step out of my comfort zone.

For most people, stepping out of our comfort zone is the most necessary and most difficult part of expectancy. For most of us, stepping out in faith is very frightening—especially the first few times that we share something from the Lord. Breaking out of familiar territory always involves risk. We risk making mistakes, embarrassment, rejection, and isolation. Some have said that we must spell faith "R-I-S-K."

I will never forget the first time that I stepped out and shared a "word." It could have been an extremely embarrassing moment if God did not come through. I was at a class that was similar to this book. We were learning to hear the voice of God for ministry. The instructor had given us a class assignment. We were to get into groups of eight and share a word of knowledge that God had given to us. Based on this word, we were to pray for the others in the group.

We all got quiet and waited for God to speak to us. As I waited on the Lord, the only word that I heard was "breast." I thought to myself, "How could I ever share this word?" Since the group was equally divided between male and female, this had the potential to be very offensive. To make matters worse, I didn't know any of these people. I had just met everyone earlier that evening. As I thought about the "word" that I had, my heart began to race. I was the last person to share. Everyone else shared very eloquent and lengthy words. All were very good. And all I had was one word—breast.

Finally, it was my turn. After about a hundred excuses why this may not be correct, I said the word "breast." To my surprise, one of the ladies in the group recently had a mammogram. The doctor had discovered a possible lump on her breast. We spent some time encouraging her. Then we gathered around her and prayed for the tumor to be removed. What could have been a very embarrassing situation became a great opportunity for powerful ministry! This would have never happened if I had not taken a risk and shared the word.

Key # 3: A Sincere Desire to Hear His Voice

Many of us have heard well-meaning Christians say that we are to seek the Giver, not the gifts. Although this statement sounds spiritual and righteous, it implies that desiring to operate in the gifts of the Holy Spirit is a wrong motivation. It suggests that the spiritual Christian should not be concerned about whether they operate in the gifts of the Holy Spirit or not. This teaching is wrong and produces passivity toward the gifts of the Spirit.

Let's look at a Scripture verse that refutes this teaching. Paul told the Corinthians, "Pursue love, yet *earnestly desire* spiritual gifts, but especially that you may prophesy." (1 Cor. 14:1). The context of this verse is 1 Corinthians 12-14, which lists the nine gifts of the Holy Spirit that we discussed in Chapter 5. The Greek word that is translated "earnestly desire" in this verse is a form of the word zeloo (dzay-lo'-o) or zeleuo (dzay-loo'-o) meaning:

- To have warmth of feeling for or against
- To burn with zeal
- To be heated or to boil with envy
- Hatred, anger (in a good sense)
- To be zealous in the pursuit of good
- To desire earnestly
- To pursue
- To strive after
- To busy oneself about him
- To exert oneself for one

This word appears twelve times in the Greek New Testament. In these verses, the word zeleuo is translated envy, covet, jealous, zealous, and desire. As we get a clearer definition of the word translated "desire," it becomes apparent that we are to have a very strong desire to hear the voice of God and to operate in the gifts of the Holy Spirit.

We know also that as we align our hearts with God, God gives us the desires of our hearts. If we desire to witness, He will give us the opportunity. If we desire to teach, He will let us. If we desire to lay hands upon the sick, He will make it happen. In the same way, if we desire to hear God's voice and minister in the gifts, He will enable us to do so.

The mindset of "I am available if you want me to minister this way" is not correct. We must ask, pray, and diligently seek to hear and minister in the gifts. I am not speaking about a lust for ministry that surpasses our desire for Jesus. The number one priority of our lives should be an intimate relationship with Jesus. However, within this context, we must earnestly desire to hear His voice and speak His words.

Key # 4: Baptism of the Holy Spirit and Praying in Tongues

The baptism of the Holy Spirit and praying in tongues help equip us to hear the voice of God and operate in the gifts of the Holy Spirit. Chapter 7 is devoted entirely to the baptism of the Holy Spirit. Chapter 8 is focused solely on praying in tongues. Since I cover these two topics in later chapters, I will only briefly mention them here.

In the New Testament, we see a connection between the baptism of the Holy Spirit and believers hearing the voice of God. For example, in the book of Acts, each time the people received the baptism of the Holy Spirit it was accompanied by some manifestation of the gifts of the Holy Spirit. In several cases, the baptism of the Holy Spirit resulted in the believers prophesying. At other times, they would speak in tongues. In the Book of Acts, the baptism of the Holy Spirit activated believers in the Hearing and Speaking Gifts. Without the baptism of the Holy Spirit, we can still prophesy or see visions; however, we cannot function in the fullness of the Holy Spirit until we experience the baptism. The reason for this is because the baptism of the Holy Spirit releases a new level of spiritual power into our lives. In later chapters, we will cover this in much more depth. For now, know that the baptism of the Holy Spirit and praying in tongues are powerful keys to hearing the voice of the Lord effectively.

Key # 5: Practice Using the Gifts

"Use it or lose it" is a common phrase that we hear in connection with the parable of the talents. In this parable, the slave who hid his talent forfeited it to the slave who had been given the most. Note this passage:

> And the one also who had received the one talent came up and said, "Master, I knew you to be a hard man, reaping where you did not sow and gathering where you scattered no seed. And I was afraid, and went away and hid your talent in the ground. See, you have what is yours." But his master answered and said to him, "You wicked, lazy slave, you knew that I reap where I did not sow and gather where I scattered no seed. Then you ought to have put my money in the bank, and on my arrival I would have received my money back with interest. Therefore take away the talent from him, and give it to the one who has the ten talents." For to everyone who has, more shall be given, and he will have an abundance; but from the one who does not have, even what he does have shall be taken away (Matt. 25:24-29).

In the Sermon on the Mount, Jesus tells His disciples not to hide their light under a basket. Note Matthew 5:14-16:

> You are the light of the world. A city set on a hill cannot be hidden; nor does anyone light a lamp and put it under a basket, but on the lampstand, and it gives light to all who are in the house. Let your light shine before men in such a way that they may see your good works, and glorify your Father who is in heaven.

The author of Hebrews tells us that our spiritual senses are trained because of practice:

> But solid food is for the mature, who because of practice have their senses trained to discern good and evil (Heb. 5:14).

Now let me summarize these three verses. In the parable of the talents, Jesus told us that if we do not use our gifts, they will be taken away and given to another who will use them. He also said that the more we use our gifts, the more we will be given. Remember, Jesus said, "For to everyone who has, more shall be given, and he will have an abundance." In His Sermon on the Mount, Jesus told us not to hide our light under a basket, but to let our light shine. Hearing God's voice and functioning in the gifts of the Holy Spirit are a way to shine our light. Finally, from Hebrews 5:14, we know that our spiritual senses are trained through practice. Putting these verses together, we can draw an important principle for hearing the voice of God:

Our skill in hearing the voice of God and functioning in the gifts of the Holy Spirit improves with practice and use. As we faithfully step out, using what we have, our skills will be sharpened.

Taking this principle deeper, our ability to operate in the gifts of the Holy Spirit will grow because of two reasons:

1. Practice
2. Faithfulness

1. Practice

As we practice using the gifts, our spiritual discernment increases. This increase operates like a weightlifter. As weightlifters work out on a regular basis, exercising their muscles, they grow stronger. Imagine what would happen if the weightlifter took three months off and then tried to lift the weight he was accustomed to. Most likely, he would not be able to lift it. Or take a football team—no football team can become championship material without practice. The team begins practicing twice a day well before the season even starts. As the old saying goes, "Practice makes perfect." This saying holds true for operating in the gifts of the Holy Spirit. The more we practice using the gifts, the more skilled and proficient we will become.

2. Faithfulness

Faithfulness is also very important to grow in the gifts. We see an example of this principle in the parable of the talents. Since the slave with the most talents was faithful, his talents increased. Additionally, the master gave him the lazy servant's talent as well. As we are faithful in small things, more will be given to us. In other words, God will give us greater gifts as we are faithful with the smaller ones. As we value and faithfully practice the gifts of the Holy Spirit, our skills will increase, and we will be entrusted with more.

KEY # 6: HUMILITY, SUBMISSION AND LOVE

Over the years of learning to hear the voice of God both for myself and for equipping others to hear His voice, I have seen the great importance of true humility, submission, and love. From my experience, these foundational character traits have a very close connection to hearing God's voice accurately. During my years in the ministry, I have encountered many wounded and angry people within the Body of Christ. No matter how the hurts were inflicted, these people often minister out of a bitter spirit. Rather than love, they minister out of anger. Rather than submission, they minister out of independence. Rather than humility, they minister out of pride. Because wounded people often have a low self-esteem, they frequently minister to others so that they feel better about themselves. The result of this type of ministry is often hard, cold, inaccurate, and destructive. Instead of drawing others closer to the Lord, ministry from a wounded spirit can push people away from the Lord, leading them into depression and discouragement.

Hearing God's voice for ministry is intended to build others up, not tear them down. It is designed to encourage and exhort others to go on with God—leading them closer to Christ. To effectively hear and minister with accuracy, power, and authority, we must be healed of past wounds and learn to walk in humility, submission, and love. We need to forgive the people who have hurt us and receive healing so that our ministry is pure and undefiled. Let us all model our ministry after Jesus who walked in humility, submission, and love.

Proficient in Hearing God's Voice

As I said at the beginning of this chapter, I encourage you to heed the six keys that we just discussed so that you can become skilled in hearing God's voice. I have equipped many people to hear God's voice by teaching these principles—so I know they work. As you give serious study to these six keys and implement them in your life, you too can be equipped to hear God's voice.

Over the years of teaching others how to hear God's voice, I have noticed two types of people. One is the person who heard the teaching and never thought much more about it after it was over. Consequently, this person never learned to hear God's voice. The second type took these principles and made them issues of prayer and fervent pursuit. This person became proficient in hearing God's voice. My prayer is that you will fit into the second category—the one who will diligently pursue learning to hear His voice! You will not regret it.

CHAPTER SEVEN

The Baptism of the Holy Spirit

As for me, I baptize you with water for repentance, but He who is coming after me is mightier than I, and I am not fit to remove His sandals; He will baptize you with the Holy Spirit and fire.

MATTHEW 3:11

But you will receive power when the Holy Spirit has come upon you; and you shall be My witnesses.

ACTS 1:8

The baptism of the Holy Spirit—what a controversial issue! This matter, along with speaking in tongues, has been one of the greatest sources of division in the Bible-believing church for the last 100 years. It makes us look at each other with doubt and skepticism. It keeps us from praying and worshipping together. It has created a great rift in the Body of Christ. Although the debate has gone on for many years, and much has been written about this subject, I include it in this book because it is an important key to hearing the voice of God. Just notice what happened to the people in the book of Acts after they received the baptism of the Holy Spirit. Among other things, they began to speak as those who knew the voice of God (Acts 2; 10:46; 19:6). When the Spirit of God fell upon believers, they were changed powerfully. The baptism of the Holy Spirit is not the only key to hearing from God, but it is an extremely important component. This chapter covers the topic of the baptism of the Holy Spirit in detail. Specifically, we will address five often-asked questions about the baptism of the Holy Spirit. It is my prayer that these answers will help us see the importance of this encounter with God.

My Journey to Spiritual Power

Before I get too deep into doctrinal issues, I want to briefly share my experience with the baptism of the Holy Spirit. In 1977, I was born-again at the age of thirty. I had a radical conversion. Before my conversion I was running away from God at full speed. When God caught up with me, He turned me around, and I have never been the same. When I was born-again, the Holy Spirit began to deal immediately with my sin. He led me to repent, to forgive, and to ask forgiveness. I began to search the Scriptures regularly to make sure that I had not committed an unpardonable sin. I wanted to know that I was truly saved. The time was a powerful one for me. The Lord put my marriage back together, restored my children, and reordered my life in virtually every area.

As I look back on my life, I know that God worked mightily through my salvation experience. For the first five years of my Christian walk, operating in the power of God was the last thing I was interested in. Although I had seen

God's power as He put my life back in order, I gave no thought to functioning in God's power myself. I was just happy that I wasn't going to hell when I died. It did not even cross my mind that I could have power to hear His voice, heal the sick, cast out demons, or teach the Word with authority. However, about five years later, my heart began to change. I started to long for God's power in my life.

I had a growing desire to do the types of works that I saw in the book of Acts. I wanted to heal the sick, cast out demons, see visions, and have spiritual dreams. I wanted what the church in Acts had. Though I knew about the baptism of the Holy Spirit, I didn't know how to receive it since the church I attended didn't teach about the baptism.

Finally, in 1983, I asked God to baptize me with the Holy Spirit. I had heard that speaking in tongues was the evidence that you were truly baptized in the Holy Spirit. Although I tried to speak in tongues, nothing happened. However, I did begin to notice more power in my life. I began to hear God's voice for ministry. Sick people that I prayed for got healed, even some from terminal illnesses.

I remember one instance very clearly. A lady in our church had terminal cancer, and the doctors gave her no hope. One Sunday before she was to have emergency surgery, I prayed for her. Sitting at the hospital with her husband, the doctor came out to give us the post operative report. He looked very puzzled as he spoke. He told us that he found no trace of the cancer. During the procedure the doctor merely corrected some problems she had in her stomach. Although this lady was only supposed to live for a few more months, she lived approximately nine more years. And her death was unrelated to her previous bout with cancer. When I performed her funeral in the early 90's, I was able to testify about God's healing power. Praise God for His healing mercy! Because the Lord baptized me in the Holy Spirit, I had the power to be used to heal cancer. Although I did not receive the gift of tongues until eight years later, I saw a definite increase in power after I prayed to receive the baptism of the Holy Spirit. From that point onward, I have seen wonderful results.

Personal Testimony or Theological Arguments

My salvation experience changed me mightily. It transformed me as it relates to *sin*. The baptism of the Holy Spirit altered my life just as much. But it transformed me as it relates to *power*. After this supernatural encounter, I received power to hear God more clearly and to perform mighty acts of healing, deliverance, and miracles.

We have heard the saying that a person with a testimony is not at the mercy of a person with an argument. This saying summarizes my attitude about the baptism of the Holy Spirit. From my own life, I know how real it is, and I know that it was a separate and distinct encounter from my salvation experience. I know that it is a necessary part in hearing the voice of God and operating in the gifts of the Holy Spirit.

Five Common Questions about the Baptism of the Holy Spirit

With this in mind, let's look at five commonly asked questions about the baptism of the Holy Spirit. As I answer these questions, I believe that God will give revelation that will help you understand and receive the baptism of the Holy Spirit. These questions are:

1. What is the baptism of the Holy Spirit?
2. What is its purpose?
3. Is the baptism of the Holy Spirit a separate experience from salvation?
4. What is the evidence that I have received it?
5. How do I receive the baptism of the Holy Spirit?

1. What is the baptism of the Holy Spirit?

The baptism of the Holy Spirit is a very significant encounter with God. It is not an optional experience for God's servants. It is not essential for some while unnecessary for others. If Jesus Himself needed the baptism of the Spirit, how much more do we? (Matt. 3:16-17). God Himself underscored its importance by recording it in all four gospels (Matt. 3:11; Mark 1:8; Luke 3:16; John 1:33). Note what John the Baptist said:

> As for me, I baptize you with water for repentance, but He who is coming after me is mightier than I, and I am not fit to remove His sandals; He will baptize you with the Holy Spirit and fire (Matt. 3:11).

The Greek word translated baptize is *baptizo*. It means to *immerse, submerge or overwhelm*. The word was not a religious term in the days of the New Testament. In fact, it was a word used in every day life. In approximately 200 B.C., Nicander, a

Greek poet and physician, used this word in a pickle recipe. He said that in order to make a pickle, the vegetable should first be dipped (bapto) into boiling water and then baptized (baptizo) in the vinegar solution. Both verbs imply the immersing of vegetables in a solution. Bapto is temporary. Baptizo, the act of baptizing the vegetable, produces a permanent change. The Greeks also used this word to describe the dipping process when a garment was permanently transformed by a dye. The Greeks also used baptizo for the drawing of water by dipping or immersing a cup into a larger vessel.

When used in the New Testament for water baptism, baptizo implies our union and identification with Christ, along with the act of immersion in water. For example, Mark 16:16 reads, "He that believes and is baptized shall be saved." Christ is saying that mere intellectual assent is not enough. There must be a union with Him—a real change—just like the vegetable is transformed into the pickle!

Not only is the baptism of the Holy Spirit a complete immersion by the Spirit, but it is also a gift from the Father to us. From the New Testament, when believers are baptized in the Holy Spirit, it is referred to as a gift. Note these Scriptures:

> Peter said to them, "Repent, and each of you be baptized in the name of Jesus Christ for the forgiveness of your sins; and you will receive the gift of the Holy Spirit. For the promise is for you and your children and for all who are far off, as many as the Lord our God will call to Himself" (Acts 2:38-39).
>
> Therefore if God gave to them the same gift as He gave to

us also after believing in the Lord Jesus Christ, who was I that I could stand in God's way? (Acts 11:17).

If you then, being evil, know how to give good gifts to your children, how much more will your heavenly Father give the Holy Spirit to those who ask Him? (Luke 11:13).

Based on these verses, here is my definition of the baptism of the Holy Spirit.

> It is a gift from God that immerses or submerges one into greater union with the Holy Spirit, resulting in a permanent change and increasing our power to be witnesses for Jesus.

2. What is its purpose?

Now that we have a working definition of the baptism of the Holy Spirit, the next question that we need to ask is, "What is its purpose?" Let's look at the Scriptures for our answer. In Acts 1:5, after His resurrection and preceding His ascension into heaven, Jesus spoke these words to His disciples: "For John baptized with water, but you will be baptized with the Holy Spirit not many days from now." Then He told them the purpose of the baptism of the Holy Spirit. Here is what He said:

> But you will receive power when the Holy Spirit has come upon you; and you shall be My witnesses both in Jerusalem, and in all Judea and Samaria, and even to the remotest part of the earth (Acts 1:8).

To help us get a clearer picture of the purpose of the baptism of the Holy Spirit, let's look at one more Greek word. The word translated "power" in Acts 1:8 is the Greek word dunamis (doo'-nam-is). It means force or miraculous power. This Greek word appears 116 times in the New Testament. In each case, it refers to the power of God working through God's servants, enabling them to do miracles, mighty signs and wonders, to bring salvation to the lost, and to establish the kingdom of God on the earth.

At the beginning of this chapter, I shared my testimony about the baptism of the Holy Spirit. Referring back to my personal experience, I will explain the purpose of this great gift from God. Earlier, I said that salvation deals with sin while the baptism of the Holy Spirit releases power. When we are born-again, we become a new creature in Christ. Old things have passed away and all things become new. We become aware of sin, conviction, and the Lordship of Jesus Christ in our lives. We begin to see our need to change. True salvation brings a tremendous transformation into the lives of most people.

Likewise, the baptism of the Holy Spirit reforms the lives of most believers by *empowering them for ministry*. After we are baptized in the Holy Spirit, we begin to sense God's leading and power in ministry. We begin to hear His voice about ministry issues. Our understanding of the Word is enhanced. And we have the power of God flowing through our lives—blessing people who need a touch from God. The baptism of the Holy Spirit releases God's power into our lives so that we can be an effective witness for Jesus Christ. It is an impartation of miracle-working power and authority enabling us to demonstrate the risen Christ to a needy world.

3. **Is the baptism of the Holy Spirit a separate experience from salvation?**

The timing of the baptism of the Holy Spirit is a major source of division in the Church. The crux of this matter is: Do we automatically receive the baptism of the Holy Spirit at the point of salvation or is it a separate event? In this section, I will answer this question and show you that these two experiences are separate events.

Although salvation and the baptism of the Holy Spirit may occur at the same time, they are separate issues and normally occur at different stages. Some have argued this point, saying that we are complete in Christ when we receive Him as our Lord and Savior. Note Colossians 2:9-10: "For in Him all the fullness of Deity dwells in bodily form, and in Him you have been made *complete*, and He is the head over all rule and authority." From the moment we receive the precious blood of Jesus, we are complete in Him because of His work on the cross. Although we have all of the blessings of Christ at the point of our salvation, we still must acknowledge what is ours and receive it by faith. Let me use a personal illustration to explain this point further.

When my youngest son, Stephen, was about one and half years old, he received many gifts at Christmas. After unwrapping numerous gifts, he announced to everyone that he was tired of opening presents. He told us that was enough and refused to open any more. Smart parents that we are, we decided to give him the remaining gifts at his birthday in March. So we took the fully wrapped, unopened presents and stored them in a closet until his birthday. When we gave him the gifts three months later, he opened them with excitement. We saved a lot of money and Stephen was blessed. From this illustration, my point is this: Stephen had all of the gifts at Christmas, but he was not able to receive them all. He reached his capacity and was content with the ones that he had opened. He didn't want anything else after that point.

The same is true with the baptism of the Holy Spirit. It is available at the point of our salvation, yet few people are able to receive it then. By far, most are content with the wonderful gift of salvation, and they do not have the capacity or understanding to receive any more gifts at that time. So God puts it up in the closet until they are ready. The gift is still theirs, reserved for them when they are able to receive it. They are not incomplete without it because it is not a badge of honor—it is a tool. Whenever the need arises, God will give it to them.

So this brings us back to our question: Is the baptism of the Holy Spirit a separate experience from salvation? My answer is a resounding "yes." It is a separate experience that requires a separate request and a separate faith. Now let's dig into the Scriptures to see if the Bible supports this premise. We will look at the Scriptures from three different perspectives to answer this question. The baptism of the Holy Spirit was a separate experience:

- In the life of the first disciples
- Every time it is recorded in the book of Acts
- As pictured in the feasts of Israel

The Baptism of the Holy Spirit Was a Separate Experience in the Life of the First Disciples

After His resurrection, the risen Lord breathed the Holy Spirit into His disciples. Look at the passage:

> So Jesus said to them again, "Peace be with you; as the Father has sent Me, I also send you." And when He had said this, He breathed on them and said to them, "Receive the Holy Spirit" (John 20:21-22).

This event was much like the Garden of Eden when God breathed into Adam, and he became a living soul. The breath of God caused Adam to come to life. In the same way, the breath of the Son of God gave new life to the disciples. They were born-again at this point. Even though they walked with Jesus for three years, participating in many miracles, they could not receive the Holy Spirit until Jesus rose from the dead. Although the Holy Spirit lived inside of the disciples, they still had not received the baptism of the Spirit. However, notice what happens approximately fifty days later on the day of Pentecost:

> When the day of Pentecost had come, they were all together in one place. And suddenly there came from heaven a noise like a violent rushing wind, and it filled the whole house where they were sitting. And there appeared to them tongues as of fire distributing themselves, and they rested on each one of them. And they were all filled with the Holy Spirit and began to speak with other tongues, as the Spirit was giving them utterance (Acts 2:1-4).

Verse 4 uses the phrase *filled with the Holy Spirit* rather than *baptized in the Holy Spirit*. However, Jesus described this same experience as the baptism of the Holy Spirit in Acts 1:5. Summarizing, the first disciples were born-again when Jesus breathed upon them, and they were baptized in the Holy

Spirit approximately fifty days later. Thus, for the first disciples, the baptism of the Holy Spirit was a separate experience from salvation.

The Baptism of the Holy Spirit Was a Separate Experience Every Time It Is Recorded in the Book of Acts
In addition to the day of Pentecost, the baptism of the Holy Spirit is described three other times in the book of Acts:

- Acts 8:12-17: Records the Samaritans receiving the Holy Spirit for the first time
- Acts 10:34-48;11:15-17: Records the Gentiles receiving the Holy Spirit for the first time
- Acts 19:1-7: Records twelve disciples of John the Baptist receiving the Holy Spirit for the first time

In each case, these people received the Holy Spirit as a separate experience from salvation. Let's discuss each example.

In Acts 8:12-17, the Samaritans first received the baptism of the Holy Spirit. Here is what happened:

> But when they believed Philip preaching the good news about the kingdom of God and the name of Jesus Christ, they were being baptized, men and women alike. Even Simon himself believed; and after being baptized, he continued on with Philip, and as he observed signs and great miracles taking place, he was constantly amazed. Now when the apostles in Jerusalem heard that Samaria had received the word of God, they sent them Peter and John, who came down and prayed for them that they might receive the Holy Spirit. For He had not yet fallen upon any

of them; they had simply been baptized in the name of the Lord Jesus. Then they began laying their hands on them, and they were receiving the Holy Spirit (Acts 8:12-17).

From this Scripture, it is easy to see that the Samaritans received the baptism of the Holy Spirit in a separate experience from salvation. They did not receive the baptism of the Holy Spirit until Peter and John arrived from Jerusalem. It is also interesting that Simon, who was traveling with them, saw that the Holy Spirit was being bestowed upon them (Acts 8:18). The baptism of the Holy Spirit was noticeable to those around. It was something that everyone could see, and it was a separate experience.

In Acts 10:34-48 and Acts 11:15-17, the Gentiles first received the baptism of the Holy Spirit. Notice what took place:

> Opening his mouth, Peter said: "I most certainly understand now that God is not one to show partiality, but in every nation the man who fears Him and does what is right is welcome to Him. The word which He sent to the sons of Israel, preaching peace through Jesus Christ (He is Lord of all) – you yourselves know the thing which took place throughout all Judea, starting from Galilee, after the baptism which John proclaimed. You know of Jesus of Nazareth, how God anointed Him with the Holy Spirit and with power, and how He went about doing good and healing all who were oppressed by the devil, for God was with Him. We are witnesses of all the things He did both in the land of the Jews and in Jerusalem. They also put Him to death by hanging Him on a cross. God raised Him

up on the third day and granted that He become visible, not to all the people, but to witnesses who were chosen beforehand by God, that is, to us who ate and drank with Him after He arose from the dead. And He ordered us to preach to the people, and solemnly to testify that this is the One who has been appointed by God as Judge of the living and the dead. Of Him all the prophets bear witness that through His name everyone who believes in Him receives forgiveness of sins." *While Peter was still speaking these words, the Holy Spirit fell upon all those who were listening to the message.* All the circumcised believers who came with Peter were amazed, because *the gift of the Holy Spirit* had been poured out on the Gentiles also. For they were hearing them speaking with tongues and exalting God. Then Peter answered, "Surely no one can refuse the water for these to be baptized who have received the Holy Spirit just as we did, can he?" And he ordered them to be baptized in the name of Jesus Christ. Then they asked him to stay on for a few days (Acts 10:34-48).

And as I began to speak, the Holy Spirit fell upon them just as He did upon us at the beginning. And I remembered the word of the Lord, how He used to say, "John baptized with water, but you will be *baptized with the Holy Spirit.*" Therefore if God gave to them the same gift as He gave to us also after believing in the Lord Jesus Christ, who was I that I could stand in God's way? (Acts 11:15-17).

From these two passages, we see that as Peter preached to the Gentiles, the Holy Spirit fell on the people. In Acts 11:16,

Peter refers to this encounter as the baptism of the Holy Spirit.

At first glance, it seems that these Gentile believers were simultaneously saved and baptized in the Holy Spirit. There does not appear to be two separate events. However, notice closely what Peter said in Acts 11:17: "God gave to them the same *gift* as He gave to us also *after believing* in the Lord Jesus Christ." Peter said that the Gentile believers received the "gift" of the Holy Spirit "after believing in the Lord Jesus Christ." Even though these two events occurred in very close proximity to one another, they are nonetheless separate experiences.

In Acts 19:1-7, Paul comes to Ephesus and meets up with twelve disciples of John the Baptist. Look at what happens when Paul is introduced to them:

> It happened that while Apollos was at Corinth, Paul passed through the upper country and came to Ephesus, and found some disciples. He said to them, "Did you receive the Holy Spirit when you believed?" And they said to him, "No, we have not even heard whether there is a Holy Spirit." And he said, "Into what then were you baptized?" And they said, "Into John's baptism." Paul said, "John baptized with the baptism of repentance, telling the people to believe in Him who was coming after him, that is, in Jesus." When they heard this, they were baptized in the name of the Lord Jesus. *And when Paul had laid his hands upon them*, the Holy Spirit came on them, and they began speaking with tongues and prophesying. There were in all about twelve men (Acts 19:1-7).

When Paul met these twelve men, he discovered that they had not yet been born-again. They had only been baptized by John the Baptist in preparation for the coming of Jesus. After learning this, Paul led them to salvation. This is implied by the phrase "they were baptized in the name of the Lord Jesus" since water baptism came after believing in Jesus' name. After leading them to salvation, Paul laid his hands on them to receive the baptism of the Holy Spirit. Again, we see salvation and the baptism of the Holy Spirit as separate experiences. After analyzing these three references in the book of Acts, I can confidently state that the baptism of the Holy Spirit is a separate experience from salvation.

The Baptism of the Holy Spirit Was a Separate Experience As Pictured in the Feasts of Israel
The three festivals that Israel has celebrated throughout history are significant to the New Testament Church. Each festival was important to the ancient agricultural society of Israel and has represented mighty truths about God to the Jews. At the same time, these three festivals paint wonderful pictures about Jesus Christ. These truths are important to the Church and should be experienced by every believer. Read Exodus 23:14-17:

> Three times a year you shall celebrate a feast to Me. You shall observe the Feast of Unleavened Bread; for seven days you are to eat unleavened bread, as I commanded you, at the appointed time in the month Abib, for in it you came out of Egypt. *And none shall appear before Me empty-handed.* Also you shall observe the Feast of the Harvest of the first fruits of your labors from what you sow in the

field; also the Feast of the Ingathering at the end of the year when you gather in the fruit of your labors from the field. *Three times a year all your males shall appear before the Lord GOD* (Ex. 23:14-17).

The emphasized words indicate that everyone should appear before God to celebrate these three festivals, and none should come empty handed. In our day, the Lord is calling many Christians to celebrate the three New Testament truths contained in these festivals. Many are celebrating Passover rather than Easter. They are observing the Fall Festival of Tabernacles as they look forward to the soon return of Jesus Christ. And they honor the birth of the Church and the outpouring of the Holy Spirit during Pentecost.

My main point is this: Every believer should encounter Jesus in all three festivals. As we celebrate Passover, we experience Jesus as our Passover Lamb whose blood has purchased our salvation. As we celebrate the Feast of Tabernacles, we anticipate the returning King by preparing ourselves for Him and His return. And we celebrate Pentecost by receiving the baptism of the Holy Spirit. Using these feasts as symbols for spiritual realities, we can see that salvation is a distinct event from the baptism of the Holy Spirit since the Feast of Pentecost is celebrated approximately fifty days after Passover.

Division between the Evangelical and Charismatic Streams
In this section, I have spent a lot of time showing why the baptism of the Holy Spirit is a separate event from salvation. I have done so for good reason. This one issue has divided the evangelical stream from the charismatic stream in the

Body of Christ. For the last one hundred years or so, this topic has created a rift of distrust, fear, and rejection. In some cases, believers from these two streams refuse even to fellowship together. Many spiritual leaders teach their people that the baptism of the Holy Spirit was given at salvation. Because of this teaching, many Christians have been robbed of the joy and power that this gift brings. If you fall into this category, I plead with you: Ask God today to baptize you with the Holy Spirit. You won't regret it!

4. What is the evidence that I have received it?

In Acts 8:18, Simon, who was following Phillip throughout Samaria, saw evidence that people had received the baptism of the Holy Spirit. Throughout the book of Acts, every time people received the baptism of the Holy Spirit, those around them knew. So the question is: *What was the evidence that someone had received it?* To answer this question, let's go to the Scriptures. Look at Acts 10:45-46:

> The circumcised believers who came with Peter were amazed, because the gift of the Holy Spirit had been poured out on the Gentiles also. For they were hearing them *speaking with tongues and exalting God.*

After these Gentiles were baptized in the Holy Spirit, they spoke with tongues and exalted God. In other passages, after the Spirit was poured out, the believers prophesied, spoke the Word of God boldly, and performed great miracles. On the day of Pentecost, Peter said that dreams, visions, and prophecy confirmed the outpouring of the Holy Spirit. Putting together the various places where the baptism of the Holy

Spirit is mentioned, the following list gives us a good idea of what we should expect:

- Prophecy
- Visions
- Dreams
- Tongues
- Desire to exalt God
- Boldness
- Gifts of the Holy Spirit (1 Cor. 12:7-11)
- Revelation and understanding

Using the list above, let me summarize my answer to this question. The primary evidence that we have received the baptism of the Holy Spirit is change. After we have received it, we will have power to love God more, power for ministry, and power to be a witness for Jesus Christ in the earth. We will also be empowered to hear God clearer, to do the miraculous works of Jesus, to gain greater understanding of the Bible, and to have an increased desire to worship the Lord. Although this is certainly not comprehensive, it does give us indicators as to whether or not we have truly experienced the baptism of the Holy Spirit. On the other hand, we might receive prayer for the baptism of the Holy Spirit and not experience any of these indicators immediately. Some people have instant results and others do not. However, as you believe in faith that you have received the baptism of the Holy Spirit, you should begin to experience some or all of these indicators at some point.

Before we end this section, let me say a few words about speaking in tongues as the evidence of receiving the baptism of the Holy Spirit. Some people say that speaking in tongues is the evidence that I have received the baptism of the Holy Spirit. Others would go on to say that if I don't speak in tongues, then I have not actually received it. My experience has been this: Tongues is an evidence but not the only evidence. As I shared in my testimony at the beginning of this chapter, I had received the baptism of the Holy Spirit for eight years before I received the gift of tongues. However, during that eight-year period, I did experience many of the other indicators that I listed above. Therefore, based on my own experience, I don't believe the gift of tongues is the exclusive indicator of receiving the baptism of the Holy Spirit.

5. How do I receive the baptism of the Holy Spirit?

Now I will answer our final question: *How do I receive the baptism of the Holy Spirit?* This is an important question. Even though we believe all of the doctrines about the baptism of the Holy Spirit, we still must experience it for ourselves. To begin answering this question, let's look at Jesus' words in Luke 11:13. He said, "God will give the Holy Spirit to those who ask." The key to receiving the baptism of the Holy Spirit is to ask for it, receive it in faith, and believe that God has done what He promised. As we ask God with a sincere heart of faith, He is faithful to fulfill His word in our lives.

After we have received the baptism of the Holy Spirit, the gift of tongues is available to us. At our church, once a person has received the baptism of the Holy Spirit, we help activate the gift of tongues in their life. However, if they do not receive tongues at this point, we tell them not to worry or fear. We encourage them by reaffirming that they have received the baptism of the Holy Spirit. We tell them that the gift of tongues will come.

I want to make one final comment about receiving the baptism of the Holy Spirit. The Scriptures refer to the laying on of hands as a component in releasing people into the baptism of the Holy Spirit. Although this is an excellent, helpful, and preferred way to impart the baptism of the Holy Spirit into someone's life, in my opinion, it is not absolutely necessary.

In summary, to be released into the baptism of the Holy Spirit, we should:

- Ask God for it
- Receive it with an open heart
- Believe in faith that you have received it
- Activate the gift of tongues by speaking out in faith

THESE PRINCIPLES WORK

I will conclude this chapter with another story from my life. Although I would not call myself a seasoned world traveler, God has given me the opportunity to minister in several places around the world. As I teach the material that we have discussed in this chapter, I have always seen powerful results. For example, in Ongole, India, I was ministering to about 120 young ministry students. The leader asked me to do a message on the baptism of the Holy Spirit. Though I had not planned to teach on this, I willingly agreed. After I was finished teaching, our team ministered to the students. Everyone in the room received the baptism of the Holy Spirit and the gift of tongues. It was a very exciting time as God poured out His Spirit. Each of these students began to experience the same things that I have seen in America, the Fiji Islands, and in Honduras. The principles from this important chapter work because the baptism of the Holy Spirit is real! Receive it today!

CHAPTER EIGHT

THE GIFT OF TONGUES

I thank God, I speak in tongues more than you all.

1 CORINTHIANS 14:18

One who speaks in a tongue edifies himself.

1 CORINTHIANS 14:4

It just rushed out of me, bypassing my mind and feeling somewhat like a flood. The ministry team of Christian International Ministries had just activated me in the gift of tongues. They were very excited, saying I was like a primed pump ready to give forth water. I was excited too. For eight years, I had been waiting for this day. Now I finally had the gift of tongues.

All along, I knew that the gift of tongues was available to me, but I didn't know how to release it. Nor did I understand the purpose of it and how it would make a difference in my walk with the Lord. However, I did know one thing—I wanted it! And now the day had arrived. I could now pray in tongues.

After receiving the impartation of this gift, I did not see

any sudden changes. I had heard many testimonies of people when they first received their gift of tongues. Some shared about waves of love engulfing them. Others shared of seeing visions. And others said they were so overwhelmed by the Holy Spirit that they could not even stand. In my case, none of this happened. It felt very good to release my spiritual language for the first time, but I didn't see visions or hear anything from the Lord. However, over time, receiving the gift of tongues has had a very significant impact on my life.

Though I have been positively affected in many ways, the greatest change came in the area of "revelation." When I say revelation, I mean God's unveiling of the Bible to me. My gift of tongues has given me much greater insight into the Word of God. Many truths of the Bible are easy to understand. We can grasp truths such as tithing, forgiveness, and repentance just by reading the Bible. However, there are other truths in the Bible that are mysteries. These truths must be unveiled. They are hidden as buried treasures, and it is our responsibility to find them and dig them out. By excavating these precious gems, we gain true knowledge and understanding. Receiving the gift of tongues opened up revelation and understanding of the Bible at an entirely new level. It brought me into the Scriptures in a much deeper way. I began to comprehend some of the mysteries that I had been blind to—even after years of studying.

The gift of tongues revolutionized my walk with the Lord—especially my devotional life and teaching ministry. Since I received the gift of tongues in 1991, I can say with full assurance that it has been an extremely powerful tool. God has used this gift to equip and empower me. Even though there were no bells and whistles when I received it, it has been a great blessing to me.

Five Common Questions About the Gift of Tongues

The gift of tongues, also known as the prayer language, is one of the most misunderstood and controversial practices in the Church. It has created much confusion and disagreement. Because of this dissension, many people without the gift of tongues don't really want it. In addition, many people with the gift of tongues don't really understand the purpose of it. With this in mind, I will discuss the gift of tongues in this chapter. I will deal with some issues related to the gift of tongues that often create fear and misunderstanding. My desire is to diffuse the lies that keep the Body of Christ from operating in this powerful gift. Just like I did in Chapter 7, I will answer five common questions about the gift of tongues. These questions are:

1. What is the gift of tongues?
2. Is the gift of tongues available to everyone?
3. Is the gift of tongues controllable?
4. Is the gift of tongues the only evidence that one has been baptized in the Holy Spirit?
5. What are the purposes of the gift of tongues?

1. What is the gift of tongues?

Let's begin answering the five commonly asked questions about the gift of tongues. Our first question is: *What is the gift of tongues?* To answer this question, I will give my definition of the gift of tongues below. It is:

> A form of spiritual communication with God that originates in our spirit, is controlled by our will, is directed by

the Holy Spirit, is normally unknown to the speaker, and leads to our edification.

To understand the gift of tongues better, let's take this definition apart and take a deeper look at some of the phrases. Our breakdown is below:

- A form of spiritual communication with God
- Originates in our spirit
- Controlled by our will
- Directed by the Holy Spirit
- Normally unknown to the speaker
- Leads to our edification

A Form of Spiritual Communication with God
The gift of tongues is *a form of spiritual communication with God*. When we pray in tongues, we are communicating with God on a spirit-to-Spirit basis. The words we speak are deeper than our native language—they are spiritual words. Paul said that the Holy Spirit prays through us with "groanings too deep for words" (Rom. 8:26). Praying in the spirit is a form of communication that transcends human words. It is at a much deeper level. This form of talking with God binds our spirit together with God's. Notice what Paul said about this: "For one who speaks in a tongue does not speak to men but to God; for no one understands, but in his spirit he speaks mysteries" (1 Cor. 14:2). When we pray in tongues, we speak directly to God.

Originates In Our Spirit
The gift of tongues *originates in our spirit*. When we are born-again, the Holy Spirit comes to reside in us. The Holy Spirit

causes our spirit-man to come alive. Note Romans 8:9-11:

> However, you are not in the flesh but in the Spirit, if indeed *the Spirit of God dwells in you*. But if anyone does not have the Spirit of Christ, he does not belong to Him. If Christ is in you, though the body is dead because of sin, *yet the spirit is alive* because of righteousness. But if the Spirit of Him who raised Jesus from the dead dwells in you, He who raised Christ Jesus from the dead will also give life to your mortal bodies through His Spirit who dwells in you.

As a born-again, baptized in the Holy Spirit believer, God has energized my spirit. Therefore, when I pray in tongues, I am speaking a spiritual language that originates in my inner man and is empowered by the Holy Spirit. Note 1 Corinthians 14:15: "For if I pray in a tongue, *my* spirit prays, but my mind is unfruitful." The gift of tongues is our spirit language, given as a gift by God.

Controlled By Our Will
We have control over the gift of tongues. In 1 Corinthians 14:15-19, Paul explains this concept to us. Notice what he says:

> What is the outcome then? *I will* pray with the spirit and *I will* pray with the mind also; *I will* sing with the spirit and *I will* sing with the mind also. Otherwise if you bless in the spirit only, how will the one who fills the place of the ungifted say the "Amen" at your giving of thanks, since he does not know what you are saying? For you are giving thanks well enough, but the other person is not edified. I thank God, I speak in tongues more than you all; however,

in the church I desire to speak five words with my mind so that I may instruct others also, rather than ten thousand words in a tongue.

We decide when to release our gift of tongues, how loud to speak it, and when to stop. Some people fear this gift because they think it is uncontrollable. They are afraid that the gift will spontaneously flow out of them at the grocery store, at work, or with family members. That is not the case at all. We have restraint over the gift of tongues. We control how and when to use it.

Directed By the Holy Spirit
The Holy Spirit directs the gift of tongues. In my opinion, this is the most valuable aspect of the gift of tongues. As we begin to speak in tongues, the Holy Spirit guides us to pray or speak what God desires in a certain situation. When we know what we are saying, our tendency is to add our own thoughts or feelings into the prayer. However, when we pray in tongues, we yield to the Holy Spirit and allow Him to pray through us whatever He wishes. Notice what Paul said about this:

> In the same way the Spirit also helps our weakness; for *we do not know how to pray* as we should, but the Spirit Himself intercedes for us with groanings too deep for words; and He who searches the hearts knows what the mind of the Spirit is, *because He intercedes for the saints according to the will of God.* And we know that God causes all things to work together for good to those who love God, to those who are called according to His purpose (Rom. 8:26-28).

Many times we don't know how to pray for a certain issue. As we use our gift of tongues, the Holy Spirit directs us how to pray. He prays through us with groanings too deep for words.

Normally Unknown to the Speaker
The gift of tongues is *normally unknown to the speaker*. Even though the gift of tongues originates from our spirit, we normally do not know what we are speaking. I use the word "normally" because there are rare occasions when we know what is said. However, far more commonly, we don't know what is being spoken. Normally, the gift of tongues is an unknown tongue.

Paul deals with this topic extensively in 1 Corinthians 12-14. This section of Scripture contains the most information about the gift of tongues in the Bible. In 1 Corinthians 13:1, in the context of speaking in tongues, Paul writes, "If I speak with the tongues of men and of angels." This implies that the gift of tongues could be either an angelic or a human language. Sometimes when we speak in tongues, humans might be able to understand what we are saying—just like on the day of Pentecost. At other times, we may be speaking a language that is known to the angels—issuing commands for spiritual warfare. However, the important point here is this: The language is normally unknown to the speaker. Paul made this clear when he wrote: "For one who speaks in a tongue does not speak to men but to God; for no one understands, but in his spirit he speaks mysteries" (1 Cor. 14:2). The speaker does not understand what he is saying because He speaks mysteries to God. Why is it so important that the language be unknown to the speaker? As we saw above, the gift of tongues helps us bypass our limited wisdom, knowledge, and understanding by allowing the Holy Spirit to pray through us the will of God.

Leads to Our Edification

The gift of tongues *leads to our edification.* Notice what Paul says about tongues and our personal edification: "One who speaks in a tongue edifies himself" (1 Cor. 14:4). When we pray in tongues, our spirit prays while our mind is inactive. This puts our mind at rest—silencing the lies, anxieties, and limited understanding that regularly bombards us. It also builds, nurtures, and strengthens our spirit; in addition, this leads to our spirit-man arising above our soul and body, and results in increased faith and intimacy with God.

Summarizing What the Gift of Tongues Is

We began this section by asking the question: *What is the gift of tongues?* Now that we have examined this definition and analyzed each aspect, let's reassemble it and summarize our answer to this question by repeating our definition. The gift of tongues is:

> A form of spiritual communication with God that originates in our spirit, is controlled by our will, is directed by the Holy Spirit, is normally unknown to the speaker, and leads to our edification.

2. Is the gift of tongues available to everyone?

The answer to this question is an emphatic "yes." The gift of tongues is available to every born-again believer who desires it. Some have debated this position by using 1 Corinthians 12:30. It reads, "All do not have gifts of healings, do they? *All do not speak with tongues*, do they? All do not interpret, do they?" I can hear the skeptics now, wondering how I will explain this one. Well, give me a moment, and I will explain why I believe this to be true.

To begin, we need to understand what Paul meant by this verse. Throughout 1 Corinthians 12-14, Paul made a clear distinction between the public and private use of tongues. The public use of tongues intended for the corporate gathering should be accompanied by an interpretation in order to edify the people. When someone speaks in tongues and an interpretation is given, it is equivalent to prophecy. On the other hand, the private use of tongues is a form of spiritual communication with God that nurtures and strengthens the spirit of the one who is praying. The private use of tongues builds us up and activates our faith. Both expressions of tongues have different purposes.

Summarizing my interpretation of 1 Corinthians 12-14, I have listed the main points below:

- If one speaks in tongues for the purpose of communicating to the gathered assembly, there should be an interpretation. Paul prefers prophecy to tongues in the public forum unless there is an interpretation. In this case, tongues and interpretation become equivalent to prophecy.

- Not everyone is gifted to move in the public delivery of a tongues message. We do not all speak in tongues in this way, do we? This is the context of Paul's statement in 1 Corinthians 12:30.

- Paul valued the gift of tongues very highly. In 1 Corinthians 14:18, Paul thanked God that he spoke in tongues more than all of the Corinthian believers. Yet he would rather speak in a known language to the church (1 Cor. 14:19).

- The individual use of the gift of tongues, also called the prayer language or praying in the spirit, is intended for every believer. In 1 Corinthians 14:5, Paul stated his desire that everyone speak in tongues. He also urged believers to earnestly desire all of the gifts (1 Cor. 12:31; 1 Cor. 14:1). In 1 Corinthians 14:13, he even told them to ask God for a gift of the Spirit that they did not have. He said, "Therefore let one who speaks in a tongue pray that he may interpret." Now if all of the gifts—including tongues—were not available to every believer, why would Paul admonish us to desire these gifts? If these gifts were not available to us, Paul would create an enormous amount of frustration by exhorting us to pursue something that we could not have.

Therefore, with all of this in mind, when Paul makes his statement in 1 Corinthians 12:30, his main point is to describe the differences in the Body of Christ, not to exclude certain believers from operating in the gift of tongues. Even though all of the gifts are available to every believer, Paul was being practical and showing the real-life scenario. Though the gift was available, not everyone had been activated to speak in tongues in a public fashion.

To further make my case that everyone can speak in

tongues, let's not forget Jesus' words when He commissioned His church:

> And He said to them, "Go into all the world and preach the gospel to all creation. He who has believed and has been baptized shall be saved; but he who has disbelieved shall be condemned. These signs will accompany those who have believed: in My name they will cast out demons, *they will speak with new tongues*; they will pick up serpents, and if they drink any deadly poison, it will not hurt them; they will lay hands on the sick, and they will recover." So then, when the Lord Jesus had spoken to them, He was received up into heaven and sat down at the right hand of God (Mark 16:15-19).

There is nothing stated or implied in this passage that only a few would speak in tongues. Rather, Jesus said that everyone who believes will speak in tongues.

Furthermore, read the four sections in the Book of Acts that offer the clearest view into the baptism of the Holy Spirit (see Acts 2:1-4; 8:5-18; 10:44-48; 19:1-7). In these accounts, we see that speaking in tongues is the most common evidence that people received the baptism of the Holy Spirit. In three of the four instances, the gift of tongues is specifically listed as a result of the outpouring of the Spirit. In the fourth case (Acts 8:5-18), a noticeable yet unidentified manifestation was observed. There is a very good chance that this could have been the gift of tongues as well.

Let me give one final illustration to support my belief that the gift of tongues is available to all who receive the baptism of the Holy Spirit. In Chapter 7, I concluded with a story about our trip to India. When we discovered that none of the students had received the baptism of the Holy Spirit or spoke in other tongues, we prayed for them. After at least an hour of ministry, every one of the students received the baptism of the Holy Spirit and the gift of tongues. To verify this, an interpreter accompanied each team member. We wanted to make sure they were speaking in an unknown tongue and not their native language. This encounter reassured me—as much as anything I have ever seen—that tongues is available to everyone who wants it.

3. Is the gift of tongues controllable?

The next question relates to the issue of control and release. Does the gift of tongues, whether public or private, just spontaneously come out of our mouth? Or do we have to release it? The answer to these questions is we have to release it. The public use of tongues is given as the Spirit wills (1 Cor. 12:11). Even though this is true, the gift of tongues does not just erupt from within our spirit. We have the ability to control it. Although it may rise up within us, we can release it or restrain it. When this gift is released depends upon whether it is public or private.

For public tongues' messages, let me share how the Spirit has led me. Though I have only been used like this a few times, each case happened in a similar way. First, I begin to sense that God wants me to deliver a tongues' message. Then the message begins to well up within my spirit. It arises within me, and I feel a burden to release it. However, I still have complete control over when I give it. I can wait until an appropriate time in the service. Or I can even refuse to deliver it, and the burden will subside. If and when I finally decide to deliver the message, the burden of the Spirit rises within me, and I release it by speaking. When I am finished, someone else delivers the interpretation in a manner similar to a prophetic word.

The individual gift of tongues must be released also. It is our gift of tongues, and we must initiate it. Both the first time we use it and each time thereafter, the exercise of the gift depends upon our activation (1 Cor. 14:14-15). Understanding that I had to release my gift of tongues confused me. Since I attended a church that did not teach us about the gift of tongues, I knew very little about it. Even though I had a strong desire for the gift of tongues, I did not know how to get it. I was waiting for God to give it to me. At times I would ask for it. At other times I would tell the Lord that if He wanted me to have it, it was okay with me. Through this approach, I never received the gift of tongues. I finally realized that it was my language given to me by the Holy Spirit. Therefore, to release it, I had to speak out. As I did this, the gift of tongues was activated in me, and I have been able to use it from that point forward. If I had continued to "wait" on God to give it to me, I still would not have this invaluable gift. We cannot just wait for the gift of tongues to come upon us. If we do this, we will most likely never be released in it. We must step out in faith in order for the gift to be activated within us.

Before concluding this section, I want to reinforce the main difference between public and private tongues. Once we have received the gift of tongues, we can use it privately whenever we wish. When we use this gift privately, we decide when to use it. This is different from the public use where the Holy Spirit prompts us when He wants to release it.

4. **Is the gift of tongues the only evidence that one has been baptized in the Holy Spirit?**

This is an important question. Although we discussed this in Chapter 7, I will talk about it here as well. Before I received the baptism of the Holy Spirit, I believed that speaking in tongues was the only sign that verified an authentic baptism in the Holy Spirit. I believed that those who did not speak in tongues were not baptized in the Holy Spirit. For a few years, I felt incomplete. I believed that God really didn't like me as much as those believers that had their gift of tongues.

Without realizing it, I viewed the gift of tongues as a test that indicated whether a person had received the baptism of the Holy Spirit. I believed that tongues was the evidence that a believer had received the baptism of the Holy Spirit. Now I realize that the gift of tongues is not a test or a sign that one has received the baptism of the Holy Spirit. The baptism of the Holy Spirit is a gift that we ask God for in faith, and the gift of tongues is not a test, but a tool. It is a tool that is extremely useful in many ways. We can use this tool in prayer, in our devotional lives and in ministry to others. God didn't give us tongues just to confirm that we have the baptism of the Holy Spirit; He gave us a valuable tool that empowers us as His witnesses in the earth.

5. **What are the purposes of the gift of tongues?**

If the gift of tongues is a tool for us to use, then what is its purpose? As I conclude this chapter, I will offer several common purposes of the gift of tongues. The gift of tongues:

- Is a means of Spirit-led prayer

- Helps us pray when we lack direction
- Helps us receive revelation knowledge from God
- Builds us up in strength and faith
- Helps us exalt God
- Empowers us in spiritual warfare
- Helps increase the amount of time that we pray

The Gift of Tongues Is a Means of Spirit-led Prayer
In Ephesians 6:18, we are told to pray in the Spirit at all times. We could easily write an entire chapter on praying in the Spirit or praying a Spirit-led prayer. Instead, I will give a brief explanation. A Spirit-led prayer, also called praying in the Spirit, is a prayer that is anointed by the Holy Spirit in accordance with the will of God. By yielding to the Holy Spirit in prayer, He helps us fulfill our call to pray according to God's will (1 John 5:14). There are two primary ways to pray in the Spirit. We can hear from the Lord what His will is and pray with our minds. Or we can use the gift of tongues, allowing the Holy Spirit to direct our prayers.

The Gift of Tongues Helps Us Pray When We Lack Direction
We all find ourselves in situations where we don't know what to pray. We can often lack direction or guidance about the way to pray. Paul talked about this to the Roman believers:

> In the same way the Spirit also helps our weakness; for we *do not know how to pray* as we should, *but the Spirit Himself intercedes for us* with groanings too deep for words; and He who searches the hearts knows what the mind of the Spirit is, because *He intercedes for the saints according to the will of God.* And we know that God causes all things to work together

for good to those who love God, to those who are called according to His purpose (Rom. 8:26-28).

From this passage, we see that the Spirit knows how to pray and will pray through us according to the will of God. Praying in the Spirit allows this to take place. When I lack direction in prayer, I have found that my gift of tongues is extremely helpful. As a pastor, people often ask me for prayer. Many times, I don't know how to pray for them. In these instances, I pray in the Spirit. As I do, God frequently gives me understanding. Taking this insight, I pray in English. By doing this, I know that I am praying God's will for the person.

The Gift of Tongues Helps Us Receive Revelation Knowledge
True wisdom from God is often concealed in mysteries. The deeper things of God are very often hidden to the natural mind. We can only perceive them through revelation knowledge. Paul told the Corinthians that the hidden mysteries of God are only revealed to us through the Spirit. Notice what he wrote:

> Yet we do speak wisdom among those who are mature; a wisdom, however, not of this age nor of the rulers of this age, who are passing away; but we speak *God's wisdom in a mystery, the hidden wisdom which God predestined before the ages to our glory; the wisdom which none of the rulers of this age has understood*; for if they had understood it they would not have crucified the Lord of glory; but just as it is written, "THINGS WHICH EYE HAS NOT SEEN AND EAR HAS NOT HEARD, AND WHICH HAVE NOT ENTERED THE HEART OF MAN, ALL THAT GOD

HAS PREPARED FOR THOSE WHO LOVE HIM."
For to us God revealed them through the Spirit; for the Spirit searches all things, even the depths of God. For who among men knows the thoughts of a man except the spirit of the man which is in him? Even so the thoughts of God no one knows except the Spirit of God. (1 Cor. 2:6-11)

Praying in the Spirit connects our spirit to God's. From this union, the Holy Spirit unlocks the mysteries of God to us. He gives us deep insight, revelation, and wisdom. He opens up the Bible and the spirit realm to us as we use the gift of tongues.

The Gift of Tongues Builds Us Up In Strength and Faith
Have you ever felt like quitting? Maybe you felt weary. Perhaps you lacked the spiritual strength and faith to continue in the call of God. During these times, the gift of tongues helps us significantly. Notice what the Bible says about this:

> One who speaks in a tongue edifies himself; but one who prophesies edifies the church (1 Cor. 14:4).

> But you, beloved, *building yourselves up on your most holy faith, praying in the Holy Spirit*, keep yourselves in the *love* of God, *waiting* anxiously for the mercy of our Lord Jesus Christ to eternal life. And have mercy on some, who are *doubting* (Jude 20-22).

The gift of tongues is a wonderful tool that helps build us up in the Holy Spirit. In my life, when I am growing weak, praying in tongues gives me fresh strength. When I feel my love for God cooling, my gift of tongues releases new passion within me. When I feel impatient or doubt attacks my mind, praying in the Spirit energizes my faith and helps me continue on in God.

The Gift of Tongues Helps Us Exalt God
Both the baptism of the Holy Spirit and the gift of tongues produce a greater desire in us to worship and exalt God. Look at three Scriptures that illustrate this truth:

> All the circumcised believers who came with Peter were amazed, because the gift of the Holy Spirit had been poured out on the Gentiles also. For they were hearing them speaking with tongues and *exalting God* (Acts 10:45-46).

> And do not get drunk with wine, for that is dissipation, but be filled with the Spirit, *speaking to one another in psalms and hymns and spiritual songs, singing and making melody with your heart to the Lord; always giving thanks for all things* in the name of our Lord Jesus Christ to God, even the Father (Eph. 5:18-20).

> What is the outcome then? I will pray with the spirit and I will pray with the mind also; *I will sing with the spirit* and I will sing with the mind also (1 Cor. 14:15).

In my life, both the baptism of the Holy Spirit and praying in tongues has enhanced my desire to worship. I used to wonder why we sang all those songs. I wanted to get straight to the message, but now I long to worship and exalt God. The gift of tongues also serves as a wonderful tool for worship. Many times, singing in the spirit enables me to express what I feel to God. This is especially helpful when I am worshipping God, and I don't know what to say or how to say it.

The Gift of Tongues Empowers Us in Spiritual Warfare
Ephesians 6:18 exhorts us to pray in the Spirit at all times. Let me make two points about Ephesians 6:18. First, this mandate is given in the context of spiritual warfare. Paul stated in verse 12:

> Our struggle is not against flesh and blood, but against the rulers, against the powers, against the world forces of this darkness, against the spiritual forces of wickedness in the heavenly places.

Also, be aware that there are two Greek words for time. *Chronos* means a space of time and *kairos* means an opportune or strategic time. Going back to Ephesians 6, Paul exhorts us to pray at those strategic, *kairos* moments. We are to pray in the Spirit at opportune times when the spiritual battle intensifies.

Let me illustrate. Many times the enemy tries to disrupt the peace in our home. He will often create strife among our children. When no amount of correction seems to help, my wife and I pray boldly using our gift of tongues with a warring attitude. When we are finished praying, peace usually returns to our home.

Praying in tongues also activates angels for spiritual warfare. Earlier in this chapter, we saw that tongues could be both angelic and human. Since the Bible says that angels are ministering spirits that render service to us, we need to activate them by speaking their language. When we engage in spiritual warfare by praying in tongues, we are actually releasing angelic commands to warring angels to fight on our behalf. Thus, the gift of tongues is a valuable tool for spiritual warfare.

The Gift of Tongues Helps Increase the Amount of Time That We Pray
Paul tells us to pray without ceasing. However, most of us run out of words to pray in a very short time. The gift of tongues helps us in this area. By praying in tongues, we can persevere in prayer, even when we don't know what else to pray for.

Tongues Is a Tool

As I conclude this chapter on the gift of tongues, I just want to reiterate the importance of the baptism of the Holy Spirit and the gift of tongues. Remember, in the Book of Acts, the baptism of the Holy Spirit and the gift of tongues activated believers in the hearing and speaking gifts. We can hear God without these valuable tools; however, they are extremely important aids that help us in the pursuit of His voice. My desire is that each of us will use the gift of tongues so as to grow stronger spiritually, have more boldness and confidence, and to hear God's voice more effectively.

End Notes

Chapter 1

1. Jack Deere, *Surprised by the Voice of God* (Grand Rapids, MI: Zondervan Publishing House, 1996), pp. 97, 114, 130, 142.

Chapter 3

1. Deere, *Surprised by the Voice of God*, pp. 323-325, 327, 330.

Chapter 6

1. Several times in this chapter, the keys to hearing God's voice are referred to as keys to moving in the gifts of the Holy Spirit. These keys apply to operating in all of the gifts, but they are especially geared toward the gifts that are activated by hearing the voice of God.

Recommend Reading

Deere, Jack. *Surprised by the Voice of God.* Grand Rapids, MI: Zondervan Publishing House, 1996.

About the Author

Ken Kessler is the Senior Pastor of Restoration Life Christian Fellowship in Marietta, Georgia. Ken and his wife Donna founded the church in 1991. Ken and Donna serve as a team, providing apostolic and prophetic vision to the fellowship. Ken is also the president of Life School International—a ministry-training center committed to making disciples in the nations of the earth. He travels throughout the world, planting the Life School in such places as India, Kenya, and Fiji.

Ken has a passion to equip believers to hear the voice of God and to minister in the gifts of the Holy Spirit. One of his greatest desires is to see the Church prepared as a worthy Bride for Jesus Christ. Ken's primary ministry goal is based on Luke 1:17: "To make ready a people prepared for the Lord." He is also dedicated to seeing a unified, city-wide Church emerge in Atlanta. Ken and his wife Donna have been married since 1969. They have four sons and two daughters in-law.

For More Information

Ken Kessler
Restoration Life Christian Fellowship
P.O. Box 671063
Marietta, GA 30066-0136
(p): 770.509.1481 (f): 770.973.6642

Email: Info@RestorationLife.org
Website: www.RestorationLife.org, or
www.LifeSchoolInternational.org, or
www.RestorationTimes.net

LIFE SCHOOL INTERNATIONAL

Life School International is a ministry training center that is dedicated to training, equipping, and releasing the Body of Christ throughout the world for effective ministry. Our vision is to disciple all nations according to Jesus' Great Commission (Matt. 28:16-20). Furthermore, we believe that the Body of Christ must be made ready as "a people prepared for the Lord" (Luke 1:17) prior to Jesus' return.

Our strategy for accomplishing our vision is to train faithful teachers that can in turn equip others (2 Tim. 2:2). We believe that leadership training is the key to fulfilling the Great Commission.

Our comprehensive, two-year curriculum involves some of the following topics:

- Understanding Your Inheritance in Christ
- Learning to Hear God's Voice
- Praise & Worship
- Healing & Deliverance
- Believers as the Bride of Christ
- The Overcoming Sons of God
- The Restoration of Israel

For more information, you can:

Go on-line at: www.LifeSchoolInternational.org

Call us at: 770.509.1481

Write us at: P.O. Box 671063
Marietta, GA 30066-0136

More Products From Restoration Times

Learning to Hear God's Voice

In *Learning to Hear God's Voice*, Ken Kessler shows us how to hear God's voice. With honesty and humor, Kessler shares real-life stories of his journey toward hearing God's voice. You will learn how to discern God's voice from the many voices that clamor for our attention; how to minister like Jesus did; and how to operate in the gifts of the Holy Spirit more effectively.

Eight Audiotapes: $40
Book: $12
Study Guide: $7

Coming in March 2004

Understanding Your Inheritance in Christ

Due for release in March 2004, *Understanding Your Inheritance in Christ* is an exciting look at how God's blessings are secured by covenant. Ken Kessler shows you how the ancient steps in covenant making apply to the New Covenant that Christ established for us; what our glorious position in Christ is; what blessings God promises to us; and how Jesus redeemed us from the curse. This book is a refreshing look at how we are called to inherit a blessing.

Eight Audiotapes: $40
Book: $12
Study Guide: $7

Developing a Heart of Bridal Love for Jesus

In this ten tape series, Ken Kessler shows how to mature as the Bride of Christ. Using Ruth as a model, you will learn how to love Jesus more than His blessings; how to remove blame and bitterness from you heart; how to develop disciplines that lead to blessings; and how to fulfill your God-given destiny.

Ten Audiotapes: $45

Watchman's Prayer Guide For Israel

The *Watchman's Prayer Guide for Israel* is a booklet containing God's wonderful covenant promises for the nation of Israel. This booklet draws exclusively from the Book of Isaiah and has almost forty pages of nothing but Scripture. It is a great aid to help you pray as watchman for the nation of Israel.

Booklet: $5

How To Order

Order On-Line: www.RestorationTimes.net

Fax Orders: 770.966.0347 or 770.973.6642

Postal Orders: P.O. Box 671063
Marietta, GA 30066-0136